OPEN TO CURE

OPEN TO CURE

Illuminating the Emotional Trauma

Expressed in Chronic Pain

Ross Halpern with David Gill

Contents

PROLOGUE

The Situation

"One cannot run away from oneself."

Sigmund Freud

BRINGING THE MIND INTO THE BODY

Change can be difficult for people. The law of inertia tells us of a resting body's tendency to remain at rest. But positive change can and does happen, and sometimes the change is massive and occurs on different levels, both personal and cultural. It often seems the change comes suddenly, out of the blue, but there is always at least a degree of momentum stimulating movement in change's direction, although often unseen, often unplanned, eventually leading to transformation. From closed to open, from confusion to understanding, from anger to joy, from slavery to freedom and as will be presented in this book, from pain to relief – all possible through courage, effort, and most importantly, a greater awareness of where one has been, and where one wishes to go.

Oprah Winfrey's sharing of her personal story of childhood sexual abuse starting when she was 9 years old, at the hands of her cousin, an uncle, and a family friend, served as a catalyst for change to both individuals and to the outdated beliefs and fears, i.e. the taboos, of our culture at large. Before this inspiring revelation to millions of people on an episode of her show in 1986, abuse was widespread, passed down from generation to generation, but hidden from view and kept secret due to shame and the long defended belief that it is "none of our business." The authority of parents, family members and caregivers to treat children however they chose went unquestioned. Police didn't interfere in domestic situations. It was considered private, not society's business. But change happened. After centuries of suffering with the dark and painful secret of childhood abuse, it was finally brought into the light, and change began to happen for millions, actually more like billions of people. Right and wrong became apparent. Taboos were challenged. Awareness of the reality of abuse and its impact on individual lives became clear. Laws changed, thinking changed, people changed.

Although the plague of cruelty to children in our culture continues, it has become nearly impossible to turn a blind eye to the reality of child abuse and its debilitating and often lifelong impact on the individuals affected. As a result of this heightened societal awareness, a helping culture has been vitalized, and victims of abuse can now avail themselves of this help and begin the process of healing the resultant pain in their lives, understanding where they have been and where they wish to go. Once light is directed toward areas of darkness, misunderstanding, and taboo, the illumination can raise awareness of what was hidden, confused, and possibly even prohibited by fears based in old beliefs and stigmas. I hope to shine a light on a situation that has been in darkness a long time.

This book explores the crisis of chronic pain in this country and attempts to reveal how the response by both the medical establishment and the suffering patients themselves is often unhelpful to the healing process. I hope to show how the attainment of greater awareness and understanding of our emotional world, and how it is expressed in physical pain, can become an invaluable tool in finding relief from that pain.

After all the tests have been done, and the medical interventions have failed, and a definitive medical diagnosis has not been found, chronic pain is inevitably treated with narcotics. This process ultimately fails to do anything but create a population addicted to opiates. Once the chronic pain patient has become addicted and also more desperate for some form of relief as the effectiveness of the drugs wane, both doctors and patients often show a greater willingness to consider a psychological approach as a possible remedy. The clinical link between physical manifestations such as chronic pain, and psychological sources such as child abuse and traumatic loss, goes back to the origins of psychology. If the repressed emotional impact of the abuses of childhood or traumatic experience at any point in one's life can be identified and brought to the patient's awareness, the unconscious and unexpressed emotional conflicts that led to its expression in bodily pain can be released.

Why then does there seem to be such an established and institutionalized avoidance of seeking a psychological intervention as the next order of business once a medical diagnosis is ruled out? Or the pain is out of proportion to the diagnosis? Why does the medical culture require the patient to wait until all the traditional medical tools

3

available fail them before considering psychological awareness as appropriate treatment? What are the obstacles within both the patient and the medical establishment to considering a deeper understanding of the pain itself as a possible cure? What is it about the possibility of an emotional source to the physical pain that feels dangerous?

It is time to challenge the status quo and the fear and misconceptions by both the medical establishment and suffering patients, of the mind's role in expressing pain. There is a need to explore the beliefs and taboos that have led to the stubborn focus on "body parts" medicine and the apparent need to find a medical diagnosis to explain the pain.

The mind is very difficult to understand. And we can't look at it with an MRI. Following the color-coded pathways of firing neurons may reveal the functions of the brain, but the mind remains elusive, and consciousness is still a mystery. But despite this reality, the mind cannot be ignored. Why is the mind important? The mind has the power to create our reality, to inform and define our experience. Its role in our experience of pain is significant whether the cause is a broken arm or a broken childhood. And because of the mind's power, along with its refusal to be dissected and viewed under a microscope, it is often left out of the discussion. At the very least it can feel intimidating and often dangerous to consider the intangible nature of the mind. Welcoming the subtle voice of the mind to the table may feel like a surrender of control. And indeed, the careful listening that is essential in hearing this voice requires an open posture. A willingness to "lose control" may be the missing ingredient in gaining relief from pain. A broken bone can be easily viewed on an x-ray, but grief, anger, trauma and anxiety cannot. The mind must be welcomed back into the body as we explore the sources and the function of our pain.

You may be thinking, "But my pain is real. I had an MRI and the doctor gave me a diagnosis. This doesn't apply to me." Yes, your pain is real, as is all pain. But if your pain just won't go away, it may be expressing more than just pressure on the nerve. It could be expressing the unconscious memory of a significant loss, a trauma, the abuse or negligence you suffered as a child. It could be made worse by guilt, grief, anxiety or anger that is too dangerous to express directly. If you feel this may apply to you, I invite you to continue in hopes that it may dispel the fears, and offer a new understanding, and provide new resources to help you cope with and possibly end your pain.

1

Obstacles

DRUGS DO NOT CURE CHRONIC PAIN

I have been a pain psychologist for over twenty years. I have evaluated and treated over ten thousand patients suffering chronic pain. I regularly work with over one hundred physicians and talk to groups of physicians and insurers who themselves provide treatment and support to patients with chronic pain. We currently find ourselves in a medical environment where chronic pain has overtaken heart disease and cancer as the number one medical problem in this country. As a result, pain is now considered a vital sign, taking its place alongside pulse, blood pressure, temperature and respiratory rate, all monitored to assess a person's general state of health.

One hundred billion dollars are spent each year in the U.S. on direct medical costs and lost productivity related to chronic pain. Beyond that, every day fifty million Americans wake up in pain and hurt all day long. At night their pain prevents a good night's sleep. Overwhelmingly, the current treatment standard for chronic pain is narcotic medication. In fact the prescribing of medication has become the medical treatment of choice for not only chronic pain, but for all medical problems, even those like diabetes and obesity, whose proper treatment is known to be a change of lifestyle such as diet and exercise.

Chronic pain is typically treated with opioid drugs such as fentanyl, hydrocodone, oxycodone and morphine. These drugs can have a short-term impact on the suppression of one's perception of pain and are particularly suited to managing pain during the recovery period following acute injury or surgery. But taking these drugs to manage chronic pain over an indefinite period of time will lead to tolerance and addiction, and ultimately they will no longer work to suppress the experience of pain, thereby leaving the patient with fewer medical options to provide relief. Chronic pain continues and the patient joins the ranks of the addicted. As bodies develop tolerance to the drugs, dosage is increased or a stronger drug prescribed with less and less pain relieving impact. Recent data reveals an ever-increasing percentage of the population in this country addicted to prescribed pain medication.

Narcotic pain medication does not cure chronic pain. You will not find a single study providing evidence of its ability to cure chronic pain, not even by the pharmaceutical companies. The successful use of these medications for intermittent pain relief, and for short-term recovery periods following injury and surgery, however, clearly identifies their value and appropriate use.

A clear distinction must be made between intermittent or occasional pain and chronic unrelenting pain. Intermittent pain is unavoidable and uncomfortable but manageable. If we fall off our bike, have a toothache, break a bone, or have surgery, pain medication can be used to quickly and thoroughly alleviate the resulting pain.

Chronic pain is a different story. By definition, chronic refers to something that doesn't go away and is generally experienced 24/7. Its intensity may waver from hour to hour or from day to day but it never ends. Instead of providing a cure, drugs prescribed to manage chronic pain create addiction. The euphemism employed to describe this phenomenon is "medical dependency," suggesting an almost tolerable result, and sounding much better than "addiction." But once addiction has set in, often accompanied by greater levels of pain, the patients find themselves referred for "rehab," essentially discarded by the medical establishment for their failure to respond to "treatment," and at this point often find their way into my office or one like it for a psychological evaluation. But the news is not all bad.

THE GOOD NEWS

There are many obstacles to gaining an understanding of the emotional components that accompany every experience of pain. These blocks exist in the culture through fear and stigma; they exist in the medical establishment through ignorance and a poorly developed referral system; and they often exist in the patient through a feeling of helplessness and shame. The often-heard question from patients, "Are you saying the pain is all in my head?" is charged with the fear of being blamed for their own pain; that it is somehow their fault. It feels dangerous to go there, to gain access to the thoughts, beliefs and emotions that may be making it more difficult to gain relief. It seems less complicated to simply get a medically based diagnosis, be prescribed a pill and be done with it. Maybe easier, but with chronic pain, never that simple.

The good news, however, is that a cure for most chronic pain does exist. And by cure, I mean cure – no more pain – restored to health – feeling good. I have seen it with my patients and with the patients of my associates. And it has nothing at all to do with drugs. The heart of the cure lays in the same treatment Oprah applied to the problem of child abuse, namely shining light on the subject. Finding the courage to open up to the unknown inner world that is our emotional life, and thus becoming aware, is the first step to finding alternative expression for the injuries and wounding that may not be as "physical" as we would hope. Does it mean the pain is in your head? No. The pain is real and it is being expressed through areas of injury and physical vulnerability.

If you suffer from chronic headaches, chronic back pain, stomach pain, or muscle pain, or any other difficult to diagnose chronic pain, it is highly likely that you fall into the category of the "curable". And that is the message I want to get to the millions of people in pain, to the millions of doctors prescribing medication, to the insurers, to the government and to the employers who are losing their employees to pain at a rate of fifty million workdays per year. "Pain management" is not what I am talking about. The key to restoring health and finding the solution to the problem of pain, is to be willing to tolerate the fear that accompanies the risk of shining enough light in the right direction so understanding can be attained.

ILLUMINATION

"Look at how a single candle can both defy and
define the darkness."
Anne Frank

Yes, the light is powerful. The eye sees nothing without
illumination. The world and its objects are imperceptible by the retina
in darkness. And likewise, the mind gains clarity and understanding
only if it knows where to look and with proper illumination. If the
light is dim or we look in the wrong direction, there may be an
adjustment in order to compensate, but this result may be an illusion
or an inaccurate interpretation. And what is it that keeps us sitting in
darkness, or looking in the wrong direction? What is the nature of
this illusion that we settle for misunderstanding over clarity?

There is a little story that you may have heard before. A man
walking home late at night from the corner tavern, having had a few
too many, discovered he was no longer in possession of his house
keys. He immediately dropped to his knees under a bright streetlight
and began crawling around searching. A fellow came walking by and
asked him what he was doing. "Looking for my keys," he answered.
"Where did you lose them?" the man asked. "Oh, back in the bar I
imagine," he said. "So why are you looking here?" said the other man.
"Well, it's dark back there, and this is where the light is."

If we want to find the real cure for chronic pain we have to look
in the right place. We have to be willing to look beyond the place that
might seem the safest or most convenient in order to illuminate the
place where the keys actually are.

BODY/MIND

Is the key to understanding the source of our pain to be found in the body or in the mind? Entertaining this question--whether the pain is a "real" physical experience in the body or something "created" in the patient's mind--is a flawed and misleading inquiry. It is a false debate based on a false premise, set into motion in the 18th century. It presumes that body and mind are two separate entities.

When we experience pain, we experience it in our bodymind, or if you prefer, our mindbody, take your pick. "Mindbody" and "bodymind" are just words. All pain is real when we experience it. If we are hurting, if we are suffering, it is real. In addition to this simple reality, it is impossible to experience pain in our body without feeling it in our mind, and it is impossible to feel pain in our mind without experiencing it in our body. Each of us is a whole person whose ongoing life experience can activate a variety of responses such as joy, sadness, or pain. These responses are highly complex reactions, not only to the sensation in moment-to-moment experience, but also to its expectation, memory, or interpreted meaning. A holistic and integrated process is triggered involving both physical and mental interactions or communications. The bodymind responds to experience at all times, sometimes with great subtlety and sometimes loudly and overtly. Our ability to allow these expressions to flow openly is complicated by our understanding or interpretation of their meaning and what we deem acceptable to us, to those in our life, or to our culture. When these reactions or expressions are blocked, whether consciously or not, they don't self-destruct; they go underground to be expressed some other way, where the blocks are less effective. The blocks to healthy expression take many forms, but often have something to do with fear, shame, guilt or anger, i.e. internalizations that may have taken root in childhood or five seconds ago. This complicated process of expression is automatic and is triggered by every experience, whether a hug from an old friend, a swim in the lake, a winning of the lottery, or a traumatic car accident; it is a process of experience and reactive expression that incorporates all that we are.

The complexity of the human bodymind is hard to understand and as a result, sometimes hard to accept, but the truth of the process being explored is becoming clearer each day.

In the last forty years there has been a veritable explosion of research conducted by scientists to understand mindbody functioning, among them physicians, biochemists, physicists, neurologists, and even biomedical engineers. Their work suggests a modern equivalent of global circumnavigation. That we experience pain in our mind when we feel it in our body and in our body when we feel it in our mind is not a theory. It is simple fact. Although not so simple considering the remarkable and nearly unfathomable complexity of the creatures we are.

EMOTIONS AND PHYSIOLOGY

With identification of a clear connection between the brain and the body's organs in the normal functioning of both the

Autonomic Nervous System and the Immune System, the biological (bodily) impact of emotional experience under conditions of extreme stress has been revealed. Emotionally based disruptions along the pathways of these normal biological processes have been found to influence the creation of a variety of chronic conditions.

An important discovery in recent research has been the impact on the body by the inflammatory responses of the immune system. As the immune system identifies and attacks pathogens in the body there is always some impact on healthy tissue in the form of inflammation. If the immune system overreacts and doesn't shut down, tissue damage can result leading to arthritis, some cancers, diabetes, Alzheimer's, heart disease, allergies, asthma, among other chronic conditions. A link between posttraumatic stress disorder (PTSD) and various somatic ailments has been observed for a long time.

Whether the emotional trauma results from a sudden unanticipated event such as a car accident, or is the result of abuse, deprivation or abandonment as a child, the impact can be severe and unmanageable. One's understanding of the experience can be conflicted by guilt and anger, or accompanied by such debilitating panic that it needs to be repressed and as a result gets expressed indirectly. Sudden overpowering loss can render the biological and emotional systems unable to cope, leading to significant expressions of pain and illness of both body and mind.

The meaning that a person brings to these traumatic events will affect how the pain is expressed. Therefore, efforts to approach the chronic pain "scientifically" must be done with care so as not to overlook the impact that the uniqueness and specificity of any one person's experience may have. To apply a standardized diagnosis and treatment plan as though one illness is just like every other is to undermine our best chance of a humane and effective cure. Psychological understanding as treatment will reveal subtle as well as significant differences from patient to patient in the meaning of the event and how it is being processed and expressed.

WHERE IS THE PAIN COMING FROM?

Despite recent findings identifying these complex interactions, the use of psychology has been much neglected as a means to effectively understand and treat chronic pain. As contemporary medicine becomes more successful and confident in its understanding of the body, it is just beginning to be more receptive to a shift in focus in its search for the key sources of chronic pain to the illumination offered by psychology. Understanding chronic pain requires going beyond the medical establishment's reliance on technical approaches to "body parts" medicine.

So let's begin with the idea that the implication in the following statement is false. "It isn't in my head; it's real physical pain." It is both, and it is impossible for it to be otherwise. The mental and emotional perception of your pain is as much a part of the experience as the sensation of the pain in your body. An important aspect has to do with yet another factor, i.e. your willingness to experience it. That seems ridiculous, doesn't it? Who would willingly submit themselves to pain?

Consider this. Let's say an event has happened and as a result of that event you are feeling pain. You are feeling it specifically in the upper part of your back, just below the shoulder on the right side. It hurts. It hurts 7 on a scale of 10. Not excruciating but definitely on the high side of painful.

Consider further these two separate situations. In the first instance, you are walking down a city street at midnight and someone you don't know walks up to you and punches you sharply and forcefully in your upper back area. In the second instance, you are lying on a massage table and the therapist has just pressed hard into the same area below the shoulder on the right side. Same place, same pain, but a different experience completely. It's easy to see that the setting, the expectation, and your willingness to experience it, all play a role in your actual sensation of pain.

So a purely "physical" pain with a purely "physical" source is affected by your "mental" response. Every event that triggers pain also triggers an emotional reaction to that pain (affecting your experience of that pain) depending on the level of fear, anger, guilt, humor, trust, acceptance or understanding accompanying the circumstance.

But this simple illustration is just the beginning of understanding chronic pain. Complications surrounding setting, expectation, willingness and interpretation are different in each situation for each person, and we haven't begun to exhaust the countless combinations affecting the human experience of pain. We will explore actual examples in greater detail in the My Casebook section of the book.

Your protests continue, "Why do we have to go into all this

psych stuff? Can't you just give me a pill?" You can take comfort in knowing you are not alone in this request. Almost half of all Americans are taking some sort of medication, millions of them for pain. Many of these people are taking combinations of drugs, pain meds, sleeping meds, anti-anxiety and anti-depression meds. The patients request it, the doctors prescribe it, and the pharmaceutical companies supply it. Sounds like a win, win, win situation, doesn't it? Is it? No, unfortunately it is not. As we are now seeing every day in the news, there are many losers in this situation, particularly many of the patients.

Drugs do not cure pain. Drugs do not cure anxiety. Drugs do not cure depression. To my knowledge there is not one company that promises that their products cure pain, anxiety or depression. Their ads will say, "manages pain" or "relieves the symptoms" of anxiety or depression. It is an open secret that cure is not expected through the use of these drugs.

Let's examine the consequences.

1. To begin with, establishing symptom relief as the only goal of treatment when cure is available isn't very smart.

2. A large percentage of our population is currently addicted to medication. And because these drugs are legal (prescribed by doctors), culturally in fashion (encouraged and supported), and promoted by the wealthiest corporations in America (marketed aggressively), the challenge of educating the market is daunting. When medication is considered the conventional response, prescribed through a carefully regulated system, what could possibly be the problem? For

starters, a third of the country is addicted to drugs. And being addicted to drugs undermines one's ability to have a fulfilling and productive life. Even worse, in the last three years more people have died of prescription drug overdose in emergency rooms than of illegal drugs.

3. The dollar cost is great. Consumers and taxpayers spend billions of dollars to pay for all those drugs. Billions of dollars are lost in the economy from "dis-abled" non-working citizens.

Okay. Who is to blame? The drug companies? The doctors? The patients themselves? Finding a place to lay blame is a national sport, if not a global sport. The market works by supply and demand. When a patient is in pain, a company will make a pill, a doctor will prescribe the pill, a pharmacy will sell the pill, all blessed and monitored by the FDA, and on the surface all appears to be well in the world. Drug companies are doing what companies do, staying in business by making profits. Doctors are doing what doctors do, writing prescriptions. Patients are doing what patients do, listening to doctors.

We need to illuminate what keeps this cycle going, and the fact that the benefits received by each of the players is out of balance. The pharmaceutical companies have the most to gain and are in fact playing a game they have little chance of losing because of their political and promotional tactics. Doctors and patients, on the other hand, although perceiving their participation in this cycle as beneficial (at least in the short term), have plenty to lose when this drug deal goes bad. Prescribing pain medication for long-term chronic pain has all the superficial characteristics associated with treatment, except for the part where the patient is cured of pain. Doctors may feel helpless when patients don't respond to surgery or some other treatment they have to offer. So as a result, pain medication is what is prescribed. Coming to the recognition that the referral of a patient to begin a psychological exploration is first order treatment, will benefit not only the patient but also the medical community itself. The patients have the most to lose in the long term, and the most to gain from illumination revealing the true sources of their pain. And doctors have much to gain in the realization that a pill, in the case of chronic pain patients, may not be the most beneficial tool in their handbag.

When chronic pain patients are referred to me for psychological treatment, they have inevitably been prescribed psychiatric meds and opiates. Family doctors and referring specialists don't have the time or training to treat someone with the proper care necessary to cure chronic pain. When no organic problem or medical diagnosis has been found as the source of the pain, psychiatric "disease" becomes the diagnosis and psychiatric medications are prescribed, along with ever increasing doses of opiate pain killers.

SETTING THE STAGE FOR AN EPIDEMIC

Cultural stigma associated with pain treatment and drugs has been on the decline since the 1950s. The stoic heroism of the WWII period led to beat generation drug experiments in the late 50s opening the door for the social revolution of the 1960s. The Vietnam War produced a generation of physically and emotionally wounded men coming home to a society that was unwelcoming and in turmoil. They treated their pain with alcohol and drugs. This new generation of fathers was less able to stow it (stoicize it) away without the help of numbing agents. Greater openness and experience with drugs along with a multimillion-dollar promotional corporate and government effort and the stage was set – for disaster.

The medicalization of psychological problems including chronic pain developed significant momentum in the early 1990s. The redirection of attention from psychosocial and therapeutic solutions to that provided by drugs was helped in part by President George H.W. Bush's friendly relationship with the pharmaceutical industry. A one-time member of the Eli Lilly (Zyprexa, Prozac) board of directors and a major stockholder, Bush supported efforts including legislation passed in the 2002 Homeland Security Act, which limited pharmaceutical company liability in litigation that claimed death or disability due to the side effects of their products. He appointed Sidney Taurel, CEO at Eli Lilly to the Homeland Security Advisory Council. {Bruce Levine, PhD, 2003} Although the power and success of these companies is old news, the devastating impact of their marketing efforts, and the relationships they cultivated in government and medicine, needs to be understood as we respond to the crisis of chronic pain and addiction today.

Although the U.S. represents only 4% of the world's population, it accounts for over 90% of all opiates prescribed. Influential doctors like Russell Portenoy, {Wall Street Journal, 12/17/12 Thomas Catan and Evan Perez} a New York pain specialist, were instrumental in promoting the use of narcotic pain medication throughout the 1990s through an exaggeration of their benefits and an understatement of the risks. This highly successful (and lucrative) promotional effort resulted in an increase of opioid sales in this country from 2 kilograms per 10,000 persons in 1998 to 7.5 kilos in 2010. {National Vital Statistics} Dr. Portenoy argued that opioids are a "gift of nature" to be employed almost indiscriminately. He felt it was his job to de-stigmatize their use. According to IMS Health, sales of opioid painkillers are approaching $10 billion a year, which is higher than the Iraq War during its costliest period.

With Medicare having directed movement of pain procedures out of hospitals in the 1990s, this country saw an explosion in the growth of new clinics dedicated to pain treatment. The efforts of Dr. Portenoy and others couldn't have come at a "better" time. With the chronic pain population growing and their receptivity to addictive narcotics at an all time high, the creation of an epidemic of addiction was assured. According to the National Institute on Drug Abuse (NIDA), there were 47,600 deaths attributed to opioid overdose in 2017, more than from all illegal drugs combined.

With a 2012 investigation by the Senate Finance Committee into the financial relationship between the pharmaceutical industry and some doctors, along with recent reporting on the frightening impact of the "opioid crisis," aggressive promotion of this gift of nature has stopped. Doctors like Russell Portenoy are no longer promoting the widespread use of opioid medications. There is a new understanding, supported by legal consequences, that narcotic painkillers are to be prescribed selectively.

2

The War on the Mind

THE 800-POUND GORILLA

There is a good reason why it is hard to believe that your pain can have roots in your psyche, i.e. in your mental and emotional life. It is because the roots, the causative roots are unconscious. They are there but you don't know it. The unconscious is the 800-pound gorilla in the room that no one acknowledges but is nonetheless running the show. Freud got it right when he identified the power of this aspect of the mind. David Eagleman uses the metaphor of an iceberg to describe the unconscious when he said, "The majority of its mass is hidden from sight." Not just some of it, but the majority of it. And like the historic iceberg that brought down the Titanic, when it remains in the darkness unseen and ignored, or worse, denied, it has the potential to cause trouble.

Bringing the unconscious into the light, looking for the keys where they actually are, is a teaching found not only in psychology, but also in all the great wisdom traditions. Socrates advised, "Know thyself." The Bible says, "The kingdom of heaven is within." Access to the unconscious and to what lies within can be found through a variety of efforts. Psychodynamic "talk" therapy, hypnotherapy, and other psychologically based therapies are not the only ways to understand one's emotional "story." The practice of meditation or focused contemplation can gradually uncover the depths of a person's inner world. Great art can reveal the unconscious at work. Sensitive bodywork can provide access to deeper inner awareness. The exploration of one's dreams can reveal through symbolic imagery the emotional energies at play in one's life. The process of coming to "know thyself" can be one of the great adventures of life; some say the greatest of adventures. Coming to understand how the unconscious is working in your life can give you access to greater freedom, greater power, and a deeper understanding of the source of your pain. And once this understanding enters your conscious awareness, you can begin to take the power back and be essentially cured of your chronic pain. Let me repeat. Gaining access to an understanding of how your unconscious is working can cure you of your chronic pain. The first step to that understanding is to open up to the adventure, to be willing to look deeper, to illuminate what lies below the surface and in the process, diffuse its destructive power over you.

This willingness is not a small thing. In fact, it is central to the process. Just as no pill will cure pain that has roots in your unconscious (no matter the dosage prescribed or how broadly it is advertised), so no psychologist or other practitioner can help you understand the impact of your unconscious without your permission and your participation in the process.

The following excerpt from Beinfield and Korngold's Between Heaven and Earth is a long one, but it's worth reading.

"...modern medicine directs its gaze through a microscope so that detail is gained at the expense of a restricted visual field. Specialists look at smaller and smaller fragments, gaining more and more positive information in the form of descriptive data but losing a sense of the integrity of the system as a whole. How did this medical model gain exclusive ascendance in America?

In the beginning of the century a survey of medical schools was subsidized by the Carnegie and Rockefeller foundations. Its purpose was to find out which schools would be most interested in promoting "scientific medicine," thereby promoting the newly developing drug- and hospital-based technology industries. The Flexner Report, issued in 1910 by the American Medical Association following this survey, recommended that financial support from the foundations be awarded only to medical schools committed to scientific research based on models developed in the 19th century. All therapies not based on the Cartesian model were considered unscientific and would therefore be disenfranchised. Only 20 percent of the existing medical schools survived (effectively eliminating all but white male participants). The other 80 percent... were ultimately driven under by lack of funds and political harassment.

Formerly the majority of physicians were helpers, allies, and comforters to people struggling with maladies in their daily life. The new doctor became the exclusive source of specialized knowledge and the heroic slayer of disease. Increasingly, a delegation of authority and power went to the doctor. Patients were educated to believe that doctors alone knew what made them sick and that only their technology or drugs could make them well...

Furthermore, as doctors became the experts, they acquired a type of power over their patients. Mastery of medicine became a technically sophisticated and exclusive high priesthood. The common person could not possibly gain access to and interpret the data necessary to administer medical care. Even the medical profession itself diversified into more highly specialized fields: the general practitioner who cared for the whole person was replaced by the cardiologist, the orthopedist, the neurologist, the oncologist... and so on.

When power was taken from the person by the general practitioner, and from the general practitioner by the specialist, there was no longer one doctor who cared for the whole person and knew her/him in the context of her/his total environment. The once intimate relationship between helper and helped shifted to an impersonal one between strangers. Doctors lost knowledge of their patients as real people.

This shift in the organization of medicine taught people to feel that science knew more about them than they could ever know or understand about themselves. People as patients began giving away the responsibility to care for their own health... People mistakenly feel that the power to cure comes from outside themselves, administered by an alien intelligence.

This distortion of power often instigates an antagonistic relationship between doctors and patients. When doctors cannot perform the heroic role and fix the broken machine, they sometimes blame the victim, judging patients guilty of not getting better. Isolated, abandoned, undermined, and invalidated, patients then feel condemned to a circle of pain with no escape. Along with their physical pain, they are frustrated and angered by their feelings of powerlessness. Then they become quick to blame the doctor for their problems, jumping into malpractice litigation. Suing for malpractice becomes an act of revenge, an attempt on the part of the patient to gain power over the doctor, not reclamation of true self-power. The doctor is either a hero or villain, heralded for recovery or blamed for poor outcomes."

The fact is that science can never know or understand more about your mind than you. Bringing the unconscious into consciousness is a process that has value beyond curing chronic pain. It is a core process for maintaining a high level of health and beyond. It is a gateway to relief from pain.

No matter how ordinary or dramatic the individual situation, knowledge of the unconscious will provide benefit in the direction of ending chronic pain. Someone who is fairly functional and is able to relate to friends and family but is suffering the daily stresses of life and has a headache or a backache that won't go away can be helped with the same process as a person whose situation may be revealed to involve the impact of greater trauma.

There are many definitions of chronic pain. I define chronic pain as pain that occurs on a regular basis, usually daily, and lasts more than three months. Some of the patients I see have had pain for three months and some have had it since they were children. I am not referring to the acute pain that occurs immediately following injury or surgery. I have worked with thousands of patients that suffer from back injuries, shoulder injuries, knee injuries, peripheral neuropathy, arthritis, headache, fibromyalgia, interstitial cystitis, pelvic pain, intercostal rib pain, chest pain, nerve damage from chemotherapy and other pain that doesn't go away.

Your situation does not need to be dramatic. Appropriate treatment is available, although not everywhere and not a lot of it, a situation I am hoping this book will begin to correct.

THE UNCONSCIOUS

The so-called unconscious isn't actually a place. You can't look at it with a microscope or an MRI machine. You can't capture it with a camera or an x-ray. But that doesn't mean it can't be experienced, observed and its impact understood. All it takes is heightened awareness and a willingness to look at oneself and one's history with new eyes or maybe just a new pair of glasses.

In trying to understand the unconscious, I think it is more helpful to think of it simply as a function of the mind that interprets our subjective experience. Our perceptions, sensations, thoughts, desires, fears, emotions, and behaviors are under constant scrutiny by the unconscious. And although we may have no awareness of the process, we respond to these ongoing interpretations of our experience with other behaviors, feelings, sensations and biological functions, i.e. various defenses to protect ourselves from danger and often the expectation of danger based in unconscious interpretations or expectations put in place a long, long time ago.

What danger you may ask? Depending on the specific nature of our experience and where we are in life in terms of our emotional and intellectual development will determine what is actually informing these unconscious interpretations. Exactly how have we experienced the world? What are the messages the world has sent in our direction? Is the world a place where we feel safe? Who is the world telling us that we are? What do we have to do and who do we have to be in order to get our needs met and feel loved?

For example, if we don't get our needs met in infancy or in childhood or if the world communicates to us that our needs are irrelevant or invalid or our voice just isn't heard, we might unconsciously interpret this experience as being our fault. If we learn that our needs and feelings are "selfish" and that what is important are the needs of our caregivers, maybe we learn very effectively to hide or disconnect from our needs and feelings. In fact, maybe we believe we are just not good enough to be loved. We may try harder and harder to please the world but if we get nowhere despite all the compensatory effort then maybe the belief that it is our fault takes root and affects us the rest of our life. Maybe as a result the unconscious interpretation leaves us feeling we should be punished for this flaw of ours. Or maybe we believe unconsciously that the only way to get a response (or to deserve a response) is be sick or in pain, so a potentially debilitating pattern develops. And in the end maybe this pattern of pain develops in our life because this is what we feel we deserve.

Unfortunately for us the unconscious interpretations of childhood are tenacious. The emotional internalizations and beliefs that develop in childhood in response to our experience of our environment and caregivers tend to get built into our personality. Without any awareness of this unconscious process these internalizations will continue to defend against the "expectation" of danger, deprivation or the unbearable feelings associated with believing you are unworthy and somehow at fault. And the sad part is that there is in fact nothing to be defended against anymore other than the beliefs themselves.

As long as we let these beliefs unconsciously run our life, the longer we will continue to provoke what we fear most. Our expectations of loss and pain run our life. We become preoccupied with finding evidence to support our ancient self-defeating beliefs. Unless we become aware of the unconscious interpretations that may have served a purpose when we were ten years old, they will continue to have power over us and to run our life. If we want the pain to stop, it is our job to take the power back, to thank the ten year old that created us (its not the other way around you know), and let them know we will take it from here. And it doesn't matter how old we are now. Wherever we are in our life right now is the perfect time to get onto the path of self-awareness, onto the path of taking the power back in order to finally end the pain. It is critical that we become aware of the unconscious workings of the mind that continue to create pain. We have suffered enough. Gaining insight into the origins and causes of these interpretations and how they have defined the limited sense of who we are, and how they continue to keep us trapped is the first step on the path to freedom and power.

It takes great courage to step onto this path. And it requires a willingness to tolerate the vulnerability that we have defended against our whole life. But as I have learned through years of professional practice, and more importantly in my own personal work to heal my own wounds, there is gold to be discovered in that vulnerability. There is power to be accessed in confronting what we fear most. And we will get there by trusting and loving ourselves, by cultivating a deep compassion for the ten year old inside us that has been doing this alone for way too long. We can begin to reevaluate the unconscious interpretations that may have been all that was available to the child and that continue to hold all the power.

WHY IS THE MIND IGNORED?

As medicine makes greater and greater progress in its use of technology, based in an advanced understanding of how the physical body functions, there is an overly confident notion that with each leap forward we get closer to the end of disease and suffering. Recent scientific medicine tracking and remapping genetic information has begun creating an expectation that all will soon be paradise. However, as patients enter my door I witness firsthand the failure of mainstream medicine, despite all it has to offer, to cure chronic pain. There appears to be a crack in the armor. As I meet with other psychologists and doctors, I am becoming more aware of a shift in this feeling of confidence. A new sentiment is being voiced that a purely physical approach to medicine may not take us where we expect. There is something missing. It is called the mind.

The knowledge of the mind provided by an MRI of the brain, today in the 21st Century, doesn't begin to compare to the knowledge of the mind offered by Sigmund Freud in the 19th Century. Just because we can look at the brain doesn't mean we understand the mind. 100,000,000,000 brain cells translate into exponentially complex networks of activity. Though neuroscientists working with MRIs have been able to map areas of the brain and determine where certain types of perception and activity may originate, one's subjective experience, however, and how it is affected by the interactions of billions of brain cells is not something that can be seen with the eyes.

The feedback loop triggered by awareness, perception, memory and interpretation and its impact on the bodymind experience represents a process infinitely too complex to capture in a snapshot. Good science requires the objective examination of the subject being studied. But consciousness cannot be examined objectively; it can only be experienced subjectively. In the scientific community this reality is ignored or denied by some and accepted by others. Despite the growth of research dollars and front-page coverage, neuroscience's fundamental inability to measure and observe subjective experience has left the subtleties of the mind and consciousness to the work of psychology. Emotions, unconscious thoughts, the experience of memory and trauma and its impact on chronic pain cannot be understood with an MRI.

THOU SHALL NOT FEEL

If only we were machines things would be so much simpler to understand and fix when broken. A little oil here, a turn of the screw there, replacing some circuitry over there, and presto, the problem is solved. Of course machines have difficult problems too. There is that little matter of nuclear reactors built on earthquake faults and computers and their viruses. Life is definitely not perfect, but all things considered, things would be a lot simpler if we were machines.

For one thing we wouldn't have feelings, those messy, often-uncomfortable whatever-they-are. We could just merrily roll around like vacuum cleaners, doing the tasks we were programmed for, on-off, no problem. And we wouldn't fall in love or wish we'd fallen in love or wake up in a bad mood. We wouldn't be angry at our boss or at our spouse or children for doing that thing again. We wouldn't feel guilty for disliking our neighbor who is trying so hard to be likeable. We wouldn't feel melancholy as summer ends. Or scared to death to read about depressed pediatric residents and their likelihood to make medication errors.

Putting the lie to the Doctor as Superman point of view, funded studies show that not only do doctors get depressed like everyone else, they in are in fact more likely to get depressed than the average person. Being a doctor ain't easy. One of the reasons for this is that doctors are under tremendous pressure in a perfectionist work culture that actually discourages them from sharing their feelings with anyone. Having feelings means you are human, and there exists an unspoken fear in the mainstream medicine culture that being too human is seen as a weakness. So feelings, which of course are based in the complexity of the mind are denied and hidden away. The effort to appear superhuman as a flawless machine is often rewarded with very human symptoms such as depression, the bodymind's reaction to being denied its status as a thinking and feeling creature.

Of course if we were unfeeling machines, the sweet experience of watching our newborn child sleep would be somehow lacking, shaving three strokes off our golf game would lose its charm, seeing our daughter get married would be so what, watching old movies or even brand new ones, even finally cleaning the closet or solving a crossword puzzle – all these would become pretty meaningless. Feelings are the vehicles through which we actually experience life. And feelings are the characteristics that link the human experience through time, past and present. We are connected to our ancestors'

31

experience through feeling. What they felt, we also feel. An actor playing a role in a Greek tragedy (or a contemporary drama) can be confident that her crying for her lost child is the expression of a feeling that was experienced in the same way two thousand years ago. In fact watching any actor playing any kind of role is enjoyable because we identify with the feelings she is expressing. There is a satisfaction in feeling the feeling, in sharing the experience with the character on the screen.

AVOIDING THE FEELINGS

If this is true, that we enjoy identifying with a character's emotional experience in a movie, why is it so hard for us to identify and understand our own emotional experience in our own life? Are we able to embrace the feeling triggered by the movie because it's really <u>her</u> feeling and not our own? Does it feel safer somehow having someone to share it with, and the fact that it's really her problem not ours? And maybe it's easier for us to feel compassion for the character than for ourselves. So rather than allowing ourselves to feel the feelings as they come up in our life, we avoid, deny, project, and mostly express them some other way, even if we don't know it's happening, especially if they are painful or complicated. Often they express themselves through physical sensations and pain in the body. Exhaustion, headaches, stomachaches, backaches, and we try to attribute the source of the pain to something "real," like a diagnosable illness. We want the doctor to identify the cause and fix it, simple as that. The possibility that it is somehow a natural reaction to anger, sadness, guilt, or some kind of emotional conflict, possibly based in old emotional wounds, often a combination of feelings we carry with us, is just unacceptable because it makes us feel powerless and out of control. We don't want it to be "our fault." But although the feeling may be too scary to feel, it will express itself one way or another. We say, "What's the point of dwelling on that old stuff? I've got to move forward in my life." But unfortunately until we do dwell on that old stuff and understand it and feel it in full awareness for the first time, it will continue to run our lives and express itself through the body, and in depression, anxiety, and often in anger.

Understanding a movie character's story, and feeling a deep sadness or a great joy in response, can be an experience of great emotional release. Imagine what it would be like to fully understand your own story and to feel the deep sadness or the great joy that is yours and only yours. Relief from pain, and freedom from fear is available if you choose to take the risk of really understanding your story.

3

I'm Not Crazy

Second only to, "Why did they send me to a psychologist, this pain isn't in my head!" is the fear expressed by thousands of my patients, the fear of being "crazy". The word triggers an image of a person living on the street, raving unintelligibly, certainly not a pretty sight nor a desirable state. Let's look at "crazy" from a few angles.

The historical angle. In late 1800s Britain, just as families were able to pay to see animals at the zoo, they could go to the Bedlam Psychiatric Hospital, pay an admission fee, and with their children, get a good look at the crazy people. At that time craziness was perceived as something that just took over a person's being; they just lost control of their mind and behavior. In other words, it was seen as an unfortunate weakness that had to be locked away, as in prison, removed from society so as not to infect or hurt the sane people, the non-crazies. Being identified as crazy was considered such a horrific thing that being referred to a psychiatrist or a psychologist was terrifying. Generationally speaking, the grandparents of many of my patients grew up in this environment of fear and stigma, and as a result, it was transferred to their children, and continues on and on.

Change is possible as understanding grows, as more people find freedom from their pain and emotional discomfort, but to this day the fear lingers. Many people that I see, interpret this referral for "psychological help" as evidence of their weakness, that they can't handle life and they fear that they will be found out. The belief that they aren't good enough, or that they're flawed, will be seen by the psychologist to mean one thing, crazy. The fear of their badness they have been running from will be exposed and confirmed, they are out of control, and it's entirely their fault. Possibly self-medicating their anxiety with alcohol or prescription drugs, they are afraid the psychologist will see right through them and have them put away. This experience of fear always creates a preference for the medical diagnosis. Degenerative this or broken that, fine, thank you, but at least I'm not crazy.

The dictionary angle. The onboard Mac dictionary defines "crazy" as "mentally deranged, esp. as manifested in a wild or aggressive way." So I looked up "deranged" and found, "to become insane; throw into confusion; act irregularly." This reference that followed was particularly interesting. "Origin late 18th Cent. French from Old French, literally, "to move from orderly rows." So I followed up with "insane" and got, "in a state of mind that prevents normal perception, behavior, or social interaction; irrational; illogical." So I checked out "normal" and read on my Mac dictionary, "conforming to a standard; usual, typical or expected."

Most people tend to want to conform to the standard of behavior and social interaction they see around them. Having at least the occasional doubt about how they may be perceived in certain situations, an effort is made, usually unconscious, to prevent the exposure of those qualities they prefer to keep in hiding. Sure, there are the brave among us like Oprah Winfrey who are willing to put themselves our there, revealing their secrets, their blemishes, their pain, moving in a new direction and in the process, creating a new normal, but they are a rare breed. Most people would rather suffer quietly in pain than reveal themselves to be out of control, to be "crazy." But the unconscious mind, just described as a giant iceberg, is hidden just below the surface, and its interpretation of our experience is running the show, and no kidding, it is realest thing in the room.

THE BIG GORILLA (AGAIN)

The unconscious is not rational and its interpretations are not necessarily in our best interest. It is simply a function of the mind limited by the resources at its disposal. Actually it is rather childlike in its literal response to the world. And its interpretations of events in early childhood tend to remain in place as the foundation of personality. These original interpretations of "reality" go very far in determining how we see the world and ourselves. Are we strong? Helpless? Defensive? Angry? Unable to receive? Is the world a safe place? Do we regularly anticipate a loving response and a positive outcome or maybe the reverse? The unconscious interpretations originating in childhood, a time we were without the resources to defend ourselves, will continue to have power in our lives, by defining who we are with or without our permission. The only way to interrupt the automatic flow of unconscious interpretation, emotion and action is to become aware, to tune in the dynamic is it plays out over and over and over creating the dominant emotional pattern of our life. To take the power back, we must see and understand.

It must be said that the unconscious mind is only unconscious to that part of us we call our conscious mind. It remembers everything that has ever happened to us, everything we have ever felt, every thought we've ever had. Part of what it does is to regulate our body without requiring our conscious participation. While we are sleeping, watching television, or while we are reading this book our body and all of its organs go on functioning without asking for our opinion or for our permission. Our conscious mind is not in control because its scope is too limited. But it is a partnership nonetheless, between the conscious and the unconscious that makes it possible for us to go about our lives from day to day.

Sometimes we take credit for what was actually the contribution of our unconscious mind, for example, a brilliant idea. Maybe we are Mozart and the brilliant idea is a fully formed sonata of great beauty. Maybe we are Bill Gates and the brilliant idea is to market a product called Windows. But maybe we are not either of those guys; we're just plain us, and the brilliant idea is to fix eggplant parmigian tonight instead of roast chicken.

Where do ideas come from anyway? A good question, and one without an easy answer. Some ideas come from our conscious mind as we shuffle and evaluate information to reach a new conclusion or solve a particular problem, and some come from the unconscious as the gorilla delivers them via dreams or in a moment of inspiration. But certainly the unconscious is always playing a role in the flavoring of our thoughts, our choices, our behaviors and our emotional interpretations, sometimes more influential and sometimes less. In the area of our emotional experience and in our experience of pain, i.e. in the area of subjective "mental" experience, the unconscious shows its dominance.

We are used to thinking that events create history – wars, discoveries, inventions – but ideas shape events and we simply don't really know where history-creating ideas come from.

Sometimes the gorilla draws attention to something that is quite other than a brilliant idea. Sometimes it comes a knocking and says, "Pay attention to this! I want you to pay attention to this! You will pay attention to this!!"

Chronic pain is like that. It functions to deliver a message that needs to be heard, that needs you to pay attention. And in the brilliant way that nature operates, pain certainly gets our attention, and often prevents us from thinking about or doing anything else.

SO WHAT NEEDS TO BE HEARD?

Pain is something we hear and feel, loud and clear. If we fall on our knee, it hurts. If someone we love dies, it hurts. If we have surgery and our body is cut, it hurts. If an important relationship ends, it hurts. We don't need any help knowing that it hurts. We feel it. Our mindbody delivers the experience both physically and emotionally. It's the energy of pain.

ARE YOU SAYING IT'S MY FAULT?

Over the years of my practice I have worked with thousands of patients who suffer from chronic pain that has no clearly definable cause. The pain will be attributed to one source or another but often there is a sense by both the doctor and the patient that something is not quite right; the degree of pain being experienced is somehow greater than what one might expect from this or that cause. Treatment in the form of pills, shots, and surgery is provided but the pain continues.

It is my certain opinion and that of many other health care providers today that a new message must be communicated and understood. I believe that chronic physical pain that has no generating cause, and although there may be a presumed "cause," is the result of unconscious emotional pain. Please read that sentence carefully. The operative word is unconscious. The emotional pain is hidden. We don't know that it is emotional. We protest, "It's not in my head. It's real pain." Of course it is real pain; all pain is real pain, but its source is often a mystery. The emotional pain is hidden. Something is creating the pain; there is pain inside of you being expressed physically. There is no doubt about its realness. But I can tell you unequivocally that it is an unconscious generator of pain and it is based in the emotions. Unconscious interpretations of experience suggesting you are unsafe, alone, at fault, or not good enough, will create pain. The gorilla has come knocking.

I would like to clarify something I call the New Age Fallacy. The idea that our mind has the ability to create pleasure or pain in our lives, is based in ancient Eastern philosophy and is generally considered to hold some truth. For example, depending upon whether we consciously respond to unavoidable life circumstances in an accepting or rejecting manner will have an impact on our experience of that circumstance. However when one considers the power and complexity of the gorilla to run our lives, and by definition, in a manner unconscious to us, "our fault" becomes a cruel and incomplete interpretation, a partial truth that adds the burden of guilt to what is already a painful situation. And guilt, or I should say a flawed interpretation of self-blame is often a key player in preventing us from expressing emotional pain emotionally rather than physically. Events in our lives, our own experience of abuse or trauma for example, are often just too unbearable to feel because of an aspect of guilt; we somehow interpret that it is our fault, so it gets expressed in physical pain. (See Chapter 5 for a detailed exploration of this unconscious conflicted dynamic, the relationship between abuse and guilt.)

Since Western medicine, aligning itself with physics, math and chemistry, generally looks for commonalities in the human race and tends to be reductionist in its outlook, the problem is reduced to the offending system, the offending organ, the offending tissue, the offending cell. And pretty much everyone with the same offending part gets the same treatment, i.e. the same "pill," mass medicine. And this is one of Western medicine's strengths. If my son gets appendicitis, you can be sure I won't take him to a psychologist; I will rush him to a hospital with physicians, anesthesiologists and surgeons, and be thankful for their expertise.

But should my son start exhibiting serious behavioral problems or become depressed or diagnosed with unexplainable chronic pain, I will bring him to the most caring psychologist I can find, because in this regard, in regard to his emotions, his behavior, and in the case of chronic pain, i.e. in regard to his hidden, unconscious emotions, he is like no one else at all. He is a unique individual among the billions on the planet, and I simply don't buy the notion that a pill or a shot would solve his difficulties. I would seek the kind of help that made it a priority to understand him, his story and his uniqueness as an individual first, before considering the relevance of any commonalities that might reveal themselves. And that is what psychology has to offer. Of course, empathy and understanding of the individual does lead to certain assumptions about the human emotional experience overall. For example, you can be sure that someone suffering chronic life-destroying feelings of low self-worth was abused, neglected, or abandoned as a child. You can be pretty sure that someone who has recently lost a loved one will be feeling the pain of grief. You can be pretty sure that someone in an unhappy relationship of many years will be feeling the pain of conflicted emotion and the resulting uncertainty. Someone who is unable to connect to the world or social interaction in a meaningful way will be feeling the pain of isolation. We are human and in many respects our hearts beat to the same rhythm.

And everyone, like my son, is unique. We share that in common; we are all unique. And because we function as individuals, we perceive stimuli and feel the complexity of emotion, based on our experience as individuals. No one experiences the "same" stimuli in the same way. Each stimulus is perceived and interpreted uniquely by each individual. In other words, all stimuli are different. For example, my sister and I grew up in the same family; however she had a brother and I had a sister. Different stimuli. Once you consider the complexity of experience based in age, gender, number of family members, order of birth, family and family member characteristics, different social situations, neighbors, babysitters, and on and on, you realize that although we are all human, each of us lives in and experiences a different world. And our unique interpretations of that world are affected by our emotional experience from moment to moment.

4

Are You Listening?

A psychologist's ability to listen represents his most valuable skill. Listening to what is being communicated both consciously and unconsciously. We communicate with words, with gesture, with emotion, and with pain. And the pain is communicating to the one experiencing the pain and to those around him. So a psychologist listens. He listens because the person in front of him matters and what is being communicated by the person matters. The psychologist listens with an empathic and a caring heart.

If you find yourself in the process of looking for a therapist (and I do recommend you take the time to make it a process, an audition process) and you feel that the therapist is not listening to you with a caring heart, I suggest you move on. If you feel unwelcome or unsafe, it may not be the best place to tell your story. If you are seeking clarity and want to understand your pain, a feeling of safety and trust are important.

Attentive and empathic listening is critical and a first step. The therapist is listening for patterns of thought, feeling or belief that may provide insight into the individual's unconscious that may not be apparent to the individual. Often internal connections are revealed that help a person understand aspects of themselves or their experience that have created an unresolved area, possibly a conflict of emotion or unconscious belief that has resulted in something difficult and maybe too painful (often unbearable) to look at (or feel) directly. Unconscious emotional conflicts often express themselves physically. Although we like to think, "Out of sight, out of mind," the reality is, as Mr. Freud said 100 years ago, we cannot escape from ourselves. Painful emotion, unless understood and to some degree, accepted as real, will express itself one way or another. Gaining awareness of the unconscious dynamics that may be causing trouble is one of the primary goals of therapy.

RELIEF THROUGH GRIEF

A client came to me with chronic head pain. He had hurt his head three years earlier falling from a ladder. He took all the tests but they could find no evidence of injury to suggest a source of pain. He was diagnosed with "Chronic pain, Unknown (cause)" and referred to my office.

"I don't know why they sent me to a psychologist," he said. "This pain isn't in my head. Well, it is in my head, but I'm not imagining it. It really hurts." I discuss mindbody connection with him and our therapy sessions proceed.

Psychotherapy is not a fifteen-minute visit. It isn't about getting a quick prescription and you're on your way. It's at the other end of the spectrum. Therapy is about the development of a relationship, a collaborative and therapeutic relationship built on trust between therapist and client. A therapist uses years of training and experience, and most importantly an intuitive empathy to help the client gain access to a new understanding of the pain. And once an understanding of the pain is revealed, the direction from which the cure may come is not far behind.

In the case of the man who fell from the ladder, we were able to establish trust soon after we began. He talked; I listened. I listened carefully with my mind, with my heart, and with my intuition. I listened for the subtle, almost invisible signs of the gorilla making himself known. You can count on the fact that the gorilla wants to be discovered. And it is knock, knock, knocking with the pain. "Pay attention to me," he says.

So I pay close attention. I listen with my third ear, so to speak. During one session the man returns to the ladder, "I had to go to the attic to get the photos we needed. And the ladder is kind of old and unsteady. I really was stupid not to use a different ladder."

"The photos you needed?" I ask.

"Yes," he said. "It's kind of embarrassing, but you see, my dad was a really great guy. He was the kind of guy who was the center of the whole extended family. Everyone really loved him a lot, not only us, but cousins, aunts, everyone. And when he died the family decided to have a huge memorial service and invite everyone he knew. And bring out all the photos of his life."

I hear the gorilla's footsteps.

"How did your dad die?" I ask gently. The emotion begins to reveal itself and he tries to push it down.

"Cerebral hemorrhage," he said. I say nothing more. Releasing his grief around the loss of his father will be a big part of this man's healing process. I witness it silently.

A couple of sessions later when I felt he had processed some of the grief that he had managed to hold below the surface and not experience directly, I said, "Maybe there is a connection between your father's sudden death from a brain hemorrhage and the pain in your head that has not stopped since your effort to look for the photos of your father's life." He looked at me. "That never occurred to me," he said. "I'll have to think about that."

Arriving at his next session he was smiling. "I had the biggest cry of my life driving home from here last week, and guess what? The headache? Gone. I woke up Tuesday and it was gone. And I don't quite believe it. First time in three years, no headache."

He continued therapy for two more weeks just to make sure. The pain was gone. He was a happy man. Case closed.

How did this happen? Well, we don't know exactly. "Exactly" as in math, chemistry, physics. In other words, we can't quantify it, measure it, replicate it, put an equation to it, or see it on an MRI. But the pain was gone. The unconscious grief had expressed itself as pain, because grief is pain, but once his grief over the loss of his father entered his conscious awareness and he accepted it for what it was, the pain could be expressed in tears and in the emotional pain of loss for someone who was loved deeply. And as a result the head pain stopped. Grief is a valid human experience and once it is accepted and expressed as such, it is allowed to evolve from an ongoing headache in my client's case, through tears into something more resembling compassion for ourselves and for those we love.

Psychology operates with a different set of rules. We know the unconscious is there, not only keeping our heart beating and our

46

body functioning without our help, but also storing away every experience we have ever had. It knows how we have been treated, it knows what we have seen, and it knows what we have been through. The unconscious and its efforts, although very difficult to understand, are involved in what I would describe as a positive process. It is attempting in its communications and expressions to maintain equilibrium of the mindbody, sometimes referred to as "homeostasis." The unconscious seeks balance and truth; it seeks reality. We can only fool it and ourselves for so long before symptoms develop. In simpler terms, the unconscious wants us to be happy or at least free to pursue happiness without the burden of pain, depression or anxiety.

5

Abuse, Trauma, Guilt = Pain

"Psychic and somatic (mind and body) phenomena take place in the same biological system and are two aspects of the same process."

Franz Alexander

Sigmund Freud referred to the movement or transition of emotional pain into a physical symptom as a "conversion." His clinical research revealed that the repression of painful memories was a potential precursor to physical symptoms often including disabling levels of pain. As described in the British Journal of Medical Psychology in 1954 by W.R.D. Fairbairn, "...conversion is a defensive technique – one designed to prevent the conscious emergence of emotional conflicts involving those (individuals) we depend on for survival. Its essential and distinctive feature is the substitution of a bodily state for a personal problem, thereby enabling the personal problem to be ignored."

It is necessary to ignore the "personal problem" because it often involves an emotion such as anger or even rage toward the person or persons depended upon for survival. Our undermining of this key relationship is interpreted as a non-option so we need to make these feelings go away so they are effectively repressed. An unconscious

48

process based in this emotional conflict begins its work. There is an assumption that it is somehow more tolerable to "convert" the emotion into illness or pain than to risk sabotaging the relationship depended upon for continued existence.

THE HARSH REALITY

Painful memories that need to be repressed can be the result of emotional and physical abuse, or trauma such as sudden devastating loss, i.e. experiences with which we were unable to cope or were too young and too powerless to even begin to comprehend. And the interpretation we come to often includes mistaken self-blame creating an intolerable emotional pain based in guilt.

For example, if the message we hear via ongoing parental abuse, neglect, rejection or shaming is that we are somehow undeserving of the care, love, nurturance and support that it is the parents' job to provide, then we inevitably blame ourselves, because we don't know any better. We are learning how the world works from the persons closest to us on whom we depend. If we don't experience the satisfaction of our instinctive needs for love and acceptance from our parents, why would we expect it from anyone else? A self-definition evolves that can include a painful sense of unworthiness, an emotional interpretation that we do not deserve love, that we are not good enough, it is our fault, we are flawed in some basic way and we are left with the understanding that we are unlovable. As a result we learn to expect rejection and mistreatment within all our relationships. The unconscious belief that we have nothing of value to offer does not however remove the need for love and acceptance. It stimulates efforts by us to compensate for this flaw in some way. Compensation can take many forms, even so far as to include a belief that punishment is the answer because it is somehow deserved. In order to survive we believe unconsciously that we will always have to do something extra. It becomes an important aspect of who we are and how we function.

If we have a self-definition built on a foundation of unworthiness we will go out of our way to find something of value to bring to the table in order to receive (or deserve) love. Overcoming the guilt of self-blame is often attempted through perfectionism or caretaking, i.e. putting others' needs before our own. Also, living with the expectation that our needs will be ignored can function in a self-fulfilling manner. An unconscious vigilance can develop that seeks evidence to support the belief that our needs will be ignored. Because this story is so familiar to us, it is somehow comforting to find the evidence, enabling us to continue employing the usual defenses and compensatory efforts, but unfortunately preventing access to the satisfaction we seek.

PAIN AS THE PERFECT COMPENSATION

Another common and effective compensation is pain, the perfect penance for the sin of unworthiness. If you are in pain, if you are suffering, then the care and love that is needed may come your way, and as a result you may survive. Keep in mind this is an unconscious process. We are blaming ourselves unconsciously, we are punishing ourselves unconsciously, and we are seeking love unconsciously.

For pain to be a suitable compensation however, it can't be of our own creation. The source or cause of the pain, must relate to something "physical" or medical, i.e. injury, illness, disease, or good old stress that is seen as resulting from carrying too great a burden, or simply having worked too hard. We seek a medical diagnosis that leaves us feeling blameless. "It is not my fault that I have fallen victim to this condition."

When psychology steps in and suggests that this expression of pain is based in an unresolved emotional conflict, the wounded self immediately takes the blame and interprets this new "mental" diagnosis as "my fault," often reinforcing the flawed sense of self that created the pain in the first place.

But if we are open to the possibility that this pain in my back, in my head, in my leg, or in my stomach might actually be an expression of emotional wounding that has found a physical vulnerability to call home, we are taking the first step toward understanding and relief. Working in relationship with a sensitive and experienced psychotherapist, the self-blame can be transformed from a belief in a flawed self into an understanding of the flawed emotional interpretation of the trauma or in the experience of abuse. The unbearable pain of feeling unloved and that it is somehow our fault can be transformed through a therapeutic reevaluation and be finally understood for what it really is.

The pain provides meaning to an empty and "faulty" sense of self. A preoccupation with physical suffering helps to distract from the unbearable experience of emotional suffering based in self-blame. Whether the pain is seen as something unconsciously deserved or simply employed unconsciously to elicit a caring response, it does the trick in taking attention away from the source. Being open to the possibility of an emotional wound (still bleeding) at the source of pain is the first step on the healing path.

TRAUMA

So what is trauma? One definition reads, "A deeply distressing or disturbing experience; emotional shock…" As per Medicine, it reads, "Physical injury." The linguistic origin of the word is identified from the Greek as "wound." A traumatized person is a wounded person.

What has the power to wound us? Lots of things, right? Life feels as though it is always ready to wound us in one way or another. The man who fell from the ladder was traumatized by the loss of his father. In this case it wasn't so-called ordinary grief that was acknowledged and experienced as almost overpowering at first but then more moderate as time went on. In this case the grief was unresolved. It was not acknowledged or accepted; it was put aside to be expressed at some other time and in some other way.

So for example, let's pretend the man who fell from the ladder has a sister. She, of course, is a unique individual like her brother and everyone else. The sister is given to expressing her emotions more directly; she is just more comfortable with emotion. She loved her dad as much as her brother did and when he died she was devastated. She cried for months and after she stopped crying she was still sad and she knew she was sad. She would say to her friends, "It's hard for me to get over losing my father." But in fact, she did get over it. She still misses him, and her life has changed because of his death, e.g. she thinks about spiritual matters more now, but as time passed, the intense hurt passed. You could describe her experience as the process of resolving the trauma of losing her father.

Her brother who fell from the ladder went through a different process. Initially he experienced grief, but it made him feel vulnerable and weak and overwhelmed. He just stopped himself from feeling. He pushed the feelings down out of his reach in an attempt to be "strong." The trauma of losing his father remained unresolved.

The old gorilla came a knocking. The man fell off his ladder "accidently," he developed pain in his head, and it wouldn't go away. Knock, knock, knock. The doctors couldn't find anything so they sent him my way. "I don't know why I am being sent to a psychologist. I'm not imagining this pain, it's real."

Yes, it is very real. It hurts to lose a father we love. And if we choose not to express it directly, through tears and depression and anger, then our bodymind will find another way. Knock, knock, knock. Our unconscious must resolve the pain. The gorilla wants us to live in balance physically and emotionally.

Until we feel it and know we are feeling it, and why we are feeling it, the gorilla will stick around doing his work. If we fully allow ourselves to feel what needs to be felt, thereby gaining access to who we are emotionally right now, if we do this consciously, the gorilla will be on his merry way. The conscious acceptance and experience of what needs to be felt and understood is what resolves pain.

The fact that physical pain, often chronic, can be caused by unresolved emotional trauma does not mean we are "crazy," or that it's "our fault;" quite the opposite. But if we are carrying internalized, unconscious beliefs based in emotional conflicts, abuse and trauma, or the experience of feeling weak, vulnerable or overwhelmed, we are in fact experiencing very real pain, and until we choose to understand its source and then express it directly, the gorilla will find a way, and we may not like what he brings us.

IDENTIFYING WHAT DOESN'T BELONG

Imagine someone in a car accident. They were in the passenger seat. The windshield is shattered and they are showered with glass. In the hospital they sedate the person and remove many small pieces of glass. But a tiny piece doesn't reveal itself and is driven deep beneath the surface. No one knows the glass is still there. The person eventually heals and goes on living. From time to time the person feels pain just below the collarbone. It hurts when it's touched. Doesn't seem like a big deal except it stays sore and then it seems to get worse, not better. What's happening?

That small piece of glass is working its way out of the body. It is rising to the surface and making itself known. The gorilla that supervises the bodymind as well as the mindbody knows that the glass has got to go. Glass in body, it concludes - not good. Before long the pain under the skin is determined to be something that doesn't belong there, the residual sliver of glass from the car accident. The person goes to the doctor and gets the glass removed. Case closed.

Unresolved emotional trauma acts like a sliver of glass hidden deep in the body. It is very painful and the bodymind wants it out.

Example. A 53-year-old woman calls for an appointment. She's had chronic stomach pain for years. Most of the time it's "just kind of low grade, but more often lately it hurts like hell." She says, "I'm a recovering alcoholic. AA saved my life. I've been in recovery six years, three months, and twenty-one days. I'm very active in the recovery community. I want to solve this pain."

"What do you mean solve?" I ask her.

"Solve," she says. "I'm pretty sophisticated about psyche stuff. The doctors can't find any cause for this pain so I know there's something emotional in there. I just can't find it." Therapy begins. She talks about her life. She talks about her marriage. She talks about her children. The therapeutic relationship develops.

"My husband is an angel. I don't know how he put up with me all those years of me drinking." She has two adult children and two grandchildren living out of state. She sees them every few months. "I'm a pretty involved grandma. I make up in quality what I can't do in quantity." She has lots of friends and sponsors many people in AA. She works part-time in a medical billing office. She says things would be great if it wasn't for the stomach pain.

"How was your childhood?" I ask.

"Normal," she says. "No problems there. We didn't have a lot of money but we weren't poor. My dad worked at Ford, and made enough money so my mom could stay home. We didn't see him all that much, he was always working, but when he was home he was a nice guy. Taught me to ride a bike and would talk to me. I have a brother and a sister. I was the middle child." And so she begins her story.

When we think about our childhood, it feels so long ago. "I'm so over that," I hear so often. "No point going back there!" But as we learned at the beginning of this chapter, our childhood creates who we are, and although it has gone underground in many cases, the reality is we are so NOT over that. The child creates the adult, not the other way around. The experiences of the child and the child's interpretations of those experiences are what create our adult selves. And until we look at and understand these experiences we are not "over" them, they are over us. But once we do revisit and come to understand the power these experiences have had in creating who we are and the pain we feel, only then can we be over them and in so doing take the power back and grow through the pain.

On the island of Aruba in the Carribbean there is a very common tree known as the divi tree. They tend to grow at a forty-five degree angle due to the constant wind blowing from the same direction on the island. Tourists that get lost are told to follow the divi trees, as they always point to the hotels.

It isn't that the divi tree would grow at this angle under all circumstances, on all islands with or without wind. It grows in this particular way on this particular island because of the wind that that is always present. Without this wind or on an island with a different wind pattern it would grow in some other way.

The experiences of our childhood are the winds that constantly blew. The "angle" at which we grew is due to the experiences of our childhood blowing us in that direction. But we are not fated to stay bent in this or that direction. We are humans, not divis. We are able to move. We look back and we can understand. We can learn, grow and change. And the pain can stop. If we want to shift our angle to this wind and change ourselves, we absolutely can.

If we experience trauma in childhood, if the wind was blowing in that direction, there is a very good chance that it went underground. As children we had to push it down and away in order to escape from its power. But this wind was so unbearable in so many cases and although we may have forgotten it, unfortunately we didn't get "over" it. It's still there and now it seems to be coming out from its hiding place where it has been all these years.

So here is our 53-year-old woman with chronic stomach pain. Why did she need to drink? What needed to be numbed and forgotten? Why was she the only one in her family who became an alcoholic? She remembers a normal, happy childhood with parents who cared and no experience of abuse. What happened? She herself has a feeling that the stomach pain is the gorilla knocking. But we can't identify what the gorilla is trying to reveal to us.

"I'm always afraid," she tells me. "I cover it real well and I'm pretty sure I started drinking to stop feeling afraid, but it didn't help. It just made things worse."

Forgetting certain chapters of childhood is not unusual. Many people struggle to remember. Experiences growing up often demand that we understand something we are not yet able to understand. Sometimes we experience or witness events that reveal something about those close to us that we can't quite accept. Misinterpretations often lead to self-blame, inevitably creating pain and denial and efforts to "put it away."

One week she came to her appointment and reported having a

very hard week. She described being "nervous as a cat" and wanting to "drink all week." The dust was rising; old feelings were asking to be addressed. It appeared that something from her past like a sliver of glass was working its way to the surface and demanding attention.

"As I was getting my regular massage, I started crying. I started crying for no reason. My therapist said that happens sometimes, that she had witnessed it before. She said emotions get trapped in the body and are released as the muscles are worked. And I've been crying all week."

I encourage her to be with the feelings, to find a way to tolerate this expression. With this kind of experience there is always the temptation to reach for the usual numbing agents before anything is learned. A fear is triggered of being overwhelmed by the unbearable feelings created by trauma in the first place. I tell her there is gold to be found in these feelings. It's where our story lies hidden. It's where we can learn who we are, and by that I mean we can learn what's been put away that to some degree has been running our life. I tell her that if she can stay with the feelings she may learn about the inner shards of glass that are finely rising to the surface. I suggest she is ready to take the power back. That she is ready to understand what has been buried and causing great pain her whole life. She leaves the session exhausted but agreeing to try.

It is often at this point that every possible effort is made to return to a state of balance, putting the gorilla back in his cage by whatever means necessary. Remaining in the vulnerable state required to access the gold is not fun. Patients will often come back with no apparent memory of what was experienced the previous session. The communication seems to be, "Everything's great (and I've gotten over that emotional episode last week)."

However, not so in this case. She returned the following week, and everything was not quite great. The slivers of emotional glass had broken through. It had all come back. She had remembered the experience from age five through nine of being sexually abused by her father. Her story unfolded, "He would come into my room and lie next to me smelling of alcohol. And he would touch me." She described the secrecy she was asked to maintain. "He said it had to be our secret so mom's feelings wouldn't be hurt. And all these years, I forgot, on purpose." The gold she had struck was painful, almost unbearably so, which explained its remaining "hidden" all these years. But now she could begin to release the tension complicated by self-blame and begin to find freedom from the pain and its expression in the body.

So the trauma, the source of the wound is finally revealed. Years of sexual abuse, and her dad not such a nice guy after all, then her struggle with alcohol and a life of fear, shame and pain. She was ready to find a resolution, to get the glass out. And create change.

But why now? What motivates the unconscious to reveal itself when it does? Why did the trauma need to be resolved at this moment? Often after years of relative stability the gorilla reveals itself. In this case, she had been sober for six years. She was in a good marriage with a supportive husband. The conditions were apparently right for her to successfully tolerate the upsurge of potentially overwhelming emotion. The human bodymind wants to heal. It makes every effort to get rid of toxins and infection-causing organisms that can do harm. Likewise, it creates the circumstances and expresses the emotions necessary to reveal and help us understand the shards of glass that we carry with us, thanks to trauma and abuse, that need to be released to enable balance and health. But we have to be ready, and we have to be paying attention, and we have to be willing to resist the temptation to numb the feelings one more time. The path to cure is initiated by looking into the pain and beginning to understand what it is trying to communicate.

6

Placebo

"The saliva of a fasting man, lozenges of dried viper, fox lungs, shed snake's skin, swallow's nest, and "the triangular Wormian bone from the juncture of the sagittal and lambdoid sutures of the skull of an executed criminal."
Medicines listed in the London Pharmacopoeia, 1621

"It may be that the symbolic armature of surgery—the shedding of blood, the cultural prestige of surgeons, even the scars that call to mind a dramatic act of healing—is itself a powerful force in recovery."
Margaret Talbot

Anyone who has read to any extent on the subject of faith or belief in medicine, known as the placebo effect, will be familiar with this story. In the 1950s, a physician named Dr. Bruno Klopfer at the University of California was treating a cancer patient we will call Mr. Wright. The patient had several large malignant tumors at various locations on his body. His prognosis was not good and Dr. Klopfer suggested he get his affairs in order. Mr. Wright had recently read in the paper an article about an apparent wonder drug named Krebiozen that was having unusual success clearing up cancerous tumors in similarly terminal patients. He brought his enthusiasm to Dr. Klopfer who was happy to comply, so treatment began. Miraculously enough, within a few days, Mr. Wright's tumors began to shrink and shortly thereafter disappeared. The patient and his family, and Dr. Klopfer were jubilant.

Weeks later a report published in the paper revealed that further research with Krebiozen was contradicting its early success and in fact was now said to be ineffective in the treatment of cancer. It was difficult news for Mr. Wright to process. He tried to ignore this new information but shortly following its release his tumors began to reappear. Dr. Klopfer, thinking about the potential impact of the news reports on both the remission and the return of the cancer reported to Mr. Wright that the drug is only ineffective at the low dose he was given. He said that at a higher dose it is proving to be effective. Mr. Wright requested and was given the higher dose.

Dr. Klopfer, who was probably on shaky legal ground, gave the patient an injection of sterile H2O. Within a few days the tumors once again disappeared. And once again all was good in the world. Unfortunately, further reports were published stating that in additional clinical trials, Krebiozen was proving to be ineffective at all dosage levels and as a result it was being withdrawn from the market. Within a week Mr. Wright's tumors reappeared and within a month he was dead.

The placebo effect is difficult to incorporate within the scientific rationalism of the medical model despite the volume of quality research proving over and over the positive effect of believing that one is being "treated" and therefore being healed. One would think a consideration of the impact of mind/emotion on disease and healing, or on pain and relief would be automatic, but despite the clear evidence provided not only in the research but also in the prevailing experience of every doctor, it is proven to be an elusive phenomenon and as a result mostly ignored by the medical world.

According to Arthur and Elaine Shapiro in their book The Powerful Placebo: From Ancient Priest to Modern Medicine, the history of medicine has been, until the last

century, a history of the placebo - creating the circumstances through setting, empathy, "medicine", surgery, or for that matter ritual chanting to produce the psychological conditions that may in themselves boost the body's own natural immune systems. A person's willingness to believe creates its own power. Belief, i.e. the placebo effect, is very difficult to incorporate in the 21st century's dominant cultural model of medicine. It can't be measured and translated into a medical treatment. Medicine used to be considered an art as well as a science, but these days there is less and less money available for art, certainly as it may relate to medicine. And it's not that hard to understand why. The roots of Western scientific medicine embraced the Cartesian philosophy and it serves to justify the ignoring of what is considered "intangible." And the mind has always been and will always be elusive in our efforts to understand its workings. Descartes said,

"All science is certain, evident knowledge. We reject all knowledge that is merely probable, and judge that only those things should be believed which are perfectly known and about which there can be no doubt."

So the illusion of certainty prevails, and intimidates those efforts that embrace doubt, intuition, and an understanding of emotion. In the old days doctors were loved for their empathy, their knowledge of the family's history of flu, measles and broken bones. Healing took place in an environment where placebo often did the heavy lifting. But we live in a new world that has no conscious tolerance of doubt or its counterpart belief.

Of course, who can blame doctors for seeking precision? Who can blame patients for expecting the same? But unfortunately, despite all the confidence and the illusion of certainty, very much is unknown. Doubt reigns but is rarely acknowledged.

A noted neurologist told me, "In some branches of medicine we know every little detail. Imagine a medical specialty as a house with many rooms and lots of furniture. In some specialties we know every little speck of that house. In neurology, we feel lucky that we know what's going on in the entrance hall."

Thirty years ago, cardiologist Bernie Siegel made a tremendous impact on health care with his book, Love, Medicine and Miracles. What he did ran contrary to most conventional medical practice. Instead of looking at the disease he looked at the people he had treated and what they were like. Specifically, he looked at those individuals who outperformed the statistics. He called them, "extraordinary patients." What characterized these extraordinary people was their belief that they would get well, that they would return to wholeness, their refusal to accept the statistical likelihood of a negative prognosis. These patients were the ones who consistently returned to health despite what their condition may have predicted.

In my practice I have seen this principle play out again and again along a range of symptoms and conditions, from minor chronic pain to the most serious of diagnoses. Openness -- to healing, to the unknown, and to an understanding of what the pain is communicating -- is the first step on the path to relief. As neuroscience makes greater and greater discoveries and advances, the enduring influence of the placebo reminds us that those things that defy measurement like belief, empathy, and a psychological understanding also endure and more importantly inspire hope, health and freedom from chronic pain.

PART TWO
My Casebook

(All patient names and specific patient circumstances
have been adjusted to protect confidentiality)

7

Secrets, Lies, and a Few Beliefs

"Pain does have a vital, lifesaving, undeniable purpose, and
that is to signal to consciousness where the problem is."
Jeanne Achterber, PhD

DAVID – CLOSER TO GOD

David was a very unusual patient. Counseling David had
elements of a mystery novel as much as a therapeutic relationship.
David is a physician who was having difficulty acting on his desire to
talk with a therapist.

"You know how it is," he said. "I don't want anyone to know I'm
seeing a psychologist."

He said he needed therapy but he didn't want to come to the
office. I felt compassion for this young man. And yes, I did know
how it is. Doctors are under tremendous pressure. Not enough time
to take care of patients properly, overwhelming paperwork, financial
and administrative problems, not to mention the constant inner
pressure to perform to the highest standard. Mistakes may be human
but they are not an option in his profession. The appearance of
relative perfection must be maintained. A fear of exposure silences
those that may benefit from seeking psychological help. There is a

belief based in reality that the medical establishment can be very hard on those who dare to reveal their humanness, in other words, their "flaws." Medicine is a scientific business; please check your emotions at the door. If one wants to advance in a superman culture, one must at least create the illusion that he or she is superman. The support that professionals could really use and benefit from and ironically help them do their job better and with greater satisfaction is most often ignored. This is the situation within which David found himself.

We arranged regular appointments over the phone. David shared his experience of fibromyalgia-like symptoms. He hurt all over and it had been getting worse for the past year.

"Tylenol worked for about a month. I saw I'd have to increase the dose if I still wanted relief. But I didn't want to, I need my liver to last a long time," he said ruefully. "I tried Lyrica and it seemed to work, but I started to gain weight. And my concentration was affected and I can't afford that. You know how it is."

"Yes," I said. "I know how it is."

"And you know how it is with these diagnoses. We don't really know what causes someone to hurt all over with no identifiable pain generator. Fibromyalgia is just a word we use. But it doesn't mean much clinically. I know you've had success with chronic pain patients so I thought I'd see if you could help me out."

"But," he continued. "This has got to be absolutely confidential. No one at the shop [the hospital] can know. I haven't even told my wife."

Over time I got to know David and his history. I learned that his was the fourth generation of doctoring in his family. And one of his sisters was also a doctor. His other sister was a lawyer. He told me that one of his earliest and most important memories was of a conversation with his great-grandfather when he was six or seven years old.

"He told me that being a doctor was a great privilege, that the relationship he had with his patients drew him closer to God. That's what he said, 'drew him closer to God.' Of course as a little boy I didn't know exactly what he meant but it had an impact nonetheless. His whole demeanor, his tone of voice, he was telling me something very important. That's when I decided I wanted to be a doctor too."

After getting this out he remained silent for a while. My job is to listen. To listen to everything I see, hear and feel. So I kept listening and he continued.

"Closer to God. Relationship to patients. What relationship? Sometimes I find myself staring at a patient's chart just to make sure I've got his name right. I feel proud of myself, and lucky, if I did. Relationship? There just isn't time."

We talked about his childhood, his mom and dad, and what it was like growing up in his family. "My childhood was like a movie. It was perfect. My parents were loving, attentive, everything. We never had money problems, not that I know of. We didn't actually talk about money. We talked about doctoring. Doctoring and science."

David had just given me a big clue.

"Perfect?" I said.

"Perfect!" he replied.

"How perfect exactly did it need to be?" I asked.

"It just was. Everything was always perfect. My dad would emphasize the importance of being 'precise,' and not making mistakes. 'If you can't do the job right, don't do it at all.' Which is hard to argue with right?" He paused as if contemplating his own question. "That's why I don't like taking the medication. It throws off my focus."

We talked about perfectionism. I asked him if he thought perfectionism was hard to argue against.

"Well, I guess when it comes to patient care and surgery it comes in handy. I sure would rather have a doctor who was a perfectionist than one who wasn't."

We talked in greater depth about the need to be perfect, and in fact it became the primary theme of our work together.

If perfect is where you must begin as well as end, what about all the learning in between? If we don't learn from our mistakes, and from taking educated risks, how do we grow as a professional and as a human being? If every effort must be perfect, and we are therefore afraid of giving it our best effort and learning from it, we become paralyzed.

It has been my observation that perfectionism is responsible for a lot of problems with pain. Often an overcompensation for unconscious feelings of being not good enough, perfection is sought to bring one's self-assessment into balance. We try to attain perfection so the feelings of low self-esteem or worthlessness don't win, because if they do we feel pain. We see it as all or nothing. But of course, perfection is impossible, and more importantly, unnecessary. Another unconscious belief that holds us hostage.

Now I must admit I too would rather have a doctor who was a perfectionist. And I would rather drive a car built by a perfectionist than not. Aesthetic beauty is also to be found in perfection. We like watching a brilliant athlete perform with perfection. We like the sound of perfectly played music. But the reality is that perfection is most often just an illusion. And perfect duplication, in products for example, eliminate the possibility of individuality and the uniqueness that so-called "flaws" create. In humans, perfection is just not possible. Even the star athlete falters. Design errors in automobiles continue to be found. Flaws are the norm. We all make mistakes from day one. And we learn as we go. If we are unable to accept the possibility of making a mistake we would be unable to do anything. We would be frozen, learn nothing and not grow.

Coming to terms with our flawed nature is a challenge I see over and over again in people with chronic pain. If we don't accept our imperfect selves, if we don't allow ourselves to be anything but perfect, if we beat ourselves up for even the smallest of mistakes, or the slightest disorder or mess creates anxiety and anger, what we get is the natural result of being beat up. We get pain.

I'm not suggesting a path of carelessness, and I think it is important to work hard and strive to do the best you can, but not to beat yourself up when you make a mistake. A sense of personal value and esteem should come from the effort, not the result. Remember, one more mistake equals one more learning experience, and that's how we grow. And our willingness to grow, to develop our knowledge, our awareness, and our skills should never stop.

If we don't allow ourselves to be human, if we can't accept the fact that we are human, if we don't let ourselves off the hook for not being perfect, the tension we feel will often end in various expressions of pain.

David began to see how his own mind was creating his pain and therefore how his mind could undo it as well. In our work together, that continued for about a year, the focus was on his effort to maintain awareness of the emotional triggers and the accompanying inner voice that would relentlessly undermine his confidence. With practice David developed the ability to actually observe the self-defeating energy as it would arise in his mind and body. By watching this dynamic he was able to create enough emotional distance, and in time diffuse its power to defeat him. He was able to report a gradually expanding experience of relief in proportion to his efforts to maintain his newly found understanding through awareness.

VICTORIA – A TARNISHED TROPHY

When Victoria came to our office, referred by her physician, everyone in the office was struck by her physical beauty. This 55-year old woman had movie star looks, the kind of physical presentation that draws everyone's attention. And with our initial conversation it was clear that she was not only physically attractive but intelligent and charming as well. She had a wry sense of humor in evidence as she talked about her experience of pain.

She had suffered back pain for years. "But frankly, Dr. Halpern," she said. "For years I didn't even realize I was in such pain, I was so pickled in alcohol." She also had regular migraines.

"I was never out of control. I never drank before lunch." She smiled a self-deprecating smile that I saw often as our sessions continued. She told me about her routine. She would wake up late and spend a few hours "putting herself together," as she called it. Then she would have lunch with friends and half a bottle of wine. "Of course once I started drinking at lunch I didn't want to break my rhythm," she said. "So lunch really just started me off. Then I'd have a wee pre-cocktail hour cocktail to keep in step. Then cocktail hour really got things going and it didn't stop till the end of the night."

"My husband loved that about me," she said. "He said I could drink like one of the boys."

Her expression changed as she mentioned her husband. "Drink like one of the boys, but a girl where it counted, he used to say."

I could see she was holding herself back from tears. "I was a trophy wife," she said. "But now I am a tarnished trophy."

Victoria had been born into a big family. She was one of six children. "We were pretty damn poor," she said. "Money was always an issue." She said she rarely saw her father. "He worked all the time and any chance he got to work more, he took it. He worked himself into the grave, died when I was 17, before I finished high school."

Of all the siblings Victoria felt she was the most blessed, "not just with looks but with smarts too." And she said she had the drive to succeed. "I was like Scarlett O'Hara. I was committed to 'never go hungry again,' just like the movie." She laughed self-mockingly. "I guess in some ways I was like my father because I worked every chance I could get when I was in high school. I was determined to go to college. I got in but after doing the math we just couldn't afford it. It took me a year to save up the balance we needed so I started a year late. But I made it!" She allowed herself a moment of triumph.

"I took an art class in my third year and one day the teacher told us he had a special treat for us. A famous art collector was visiting the school and would grace us with a special talk. And in the evening we were all invited to a reception in his honor. It was all very thrilling to me. I thought this famous art collector would be some old man but he turned out to be in his thirties, and very handsome. He dressed like a rich man, what looked like very expensive designer clothes. I was already interested in fashion. He was funny and he gave a good talk."

She continued, "Anyway, he chatted with me during the reception and told me that he would be back in town in a few weeks and he'd like to take me to dinner and would I like to do that? Wow! I think those were the most nervous three weeks of my life!

"He took me to a restaurant that we had to drive an hour to get to. I had never been in such a place. We had our own private little room. The menu didn't have prices on it. I'll never forget that.

"And he was a complete gentleman. Took me right home afterwards, didn't try anything. He courted me for about a month. I was madly in love! And then he asked me to marry him!

"Well, of course I did. How could I not? He was nice, he was romantic, he was rich, and I was in love. My mother was thrilled. My family couldn't believe it. It was like a movie.

"I quit school and just traveled around with him. He traveled a lot. I would travel with him and hang around the hotel waiting for him to come back from his meetings. Sometimes I would shop or visit museums but most of the time I just stayed in the hotel.

"He actually would introduce me as his trophy, you know making a joke. We didn't have children. He didn't want them and I wanted what he wanted.

"After about ten years I stayed home. I was tired of hanging around hotels. And he'd started coming back to the hotel later and later, and then he would fall asleep. It was pointless for me to go with him, he said.

"So I stayed home and kept shopping and going to lunch with my friends and basically getting loaded every afternoon and evening and falling asleep in front of the TV. There isn't a movie made that I haven't seen," she said with a self-mocking laugh. "My friends would want to introduce me to men but I wouldn't have it. I was married and in love with my husband.

"So finally, one day he came home from a trip and took me to a restaurant we hadn't been to in years. It was a beautiful place, very quiet and discreet. He said to me, and I'll never forget this, 'Victoria, I don't know how to say this, so I'll just say it. I want a divorce.'

"Bam! Just like that. Out of nowhere. But of course I knew it wasn't out of nowhere. It had been coming for years but I was too stupid to see it.

"I was demolished. I couldn't say a thing. I couldn't respond in any way. I remember drifting out of the restaurant and feeling numb all the way home. After that I barely saw him at all. I learned through a friend of a friend's husband that he had been seeing someone else for three years and she was about the same age as I was when we met. I guess he wanted a newer model trophy."

Victoria was in pain as she told the story, but she maintained her rueful smile.

"The divorce went quick. I didn't fight. I was too used to giving him what he wanted. And I still loved him. I got enough money so I wouldn't have to work. I could just continue sitting in front of the TV getting loaded. Only I stopped waiting until lunch to start drinking. Finally it got so bad that my friends intervened, thank God. They told me I had to stop. They helped me arrange a rehab visit for three weeks and I have continued with AA since then. And it worked. But then one year later my mom died. And then my back went out and the migraines started. I guess I can't get a break."

She told me the medications she was taking. Drugs to ease the pain, to relax her, and to help her sleep.

"Does it relieve the pain?" I asked.

"Sometimes," she said, "but nothing helps the migraines. I just lie in the dark sometimes all day."

"Does it help you sleep?" I asked.

"It did for awhile."

"And does it help you relax?"

She laughed bitterly. "Relax? I just live for my Valium. It's the only thing in my life that's working. It makes me feel decent. I'm 55 and I'll never find another man like my husband, regardless how bad he treated me. I was useless then and I'm useless now. And I hurt. My back hurts, my head hurts. No, I am not relaxed. That doesn't seem to describe what I am."

We started regular therapy. We focused the work on her feelings of grief, betrayal, and anger complicated by self-blame that she never allowed herself to feel. The work in therapy revealed that her relationship with her husband was in many ways similar to her relationship with her father. Her husband, like her father was always working. She rarely saw either of them. And she interpreted their absence as a sign of their love. They were always working to make her life better. She felt rescued in different ways by both of them. She trusted them both. And when her father died when she was only 17, she was never able to allow herself to grieve. She never accepted the loss, and then threw herself into schoolwork and her efforts to "never go hungry again." When she met her husband, she felt soothed and taken care of, and unconsciously it felt like a reconnection to her father. So she didn't fight it. She became passive, and numb, and she "loved" him. And then it was over. It brought back the feelings of loss and grief that were never fully expressed when she was 17. Grief and anger were trapped in her body, being expressed in migraine headaches and back pain. With her new awareness and the understanding revealed in therapy, the emotional numbness she was feeling broke through into a direct expression of deep sadness and the beginning of the process leading to self-forgiveness. She was suffering great loss and she blamed herself. She was now able to feel the grief of losing not only her husband but also her father. She was also able to find the more appropriate target for the anger she was feeling in being abandoned by her husband. Her breakthrough was revealed with one word.

"Bastard," she said.

She had hit the target, and with the flowing tears that followed she felt the beginnings of relief from the unbearable pain of self-blame. Her feelings were understood and were now being expressed directly. There would no more need for migraines, or for that matter, the medication.

Within a few weeks Victoria came to session and told me she would like to get off the pills. She said, "It's getting near Thanksgiving and I'm thinking of going cold turkey."

I suggested she wait and consult with a drug dependency physician to help her get off the medication safely. Discontinuing narcotic medications can be brutal, even dangerous, and it is best done under the close supervision of a specialist. I referred Victoria to someone I consider one of the best in this area and as a result she has been able to get back on the path to a state of mindbody health. We continued to work together for about six months. She was able to get off the medication safely, her back pain became more of what she described as an "occasional discomfort," and her insomnia was resolved. Through the emotional work of feeling the feelings and accepting her story, she was able to develop the inner resources and the awareness required to stop the pain.

ALOHA – TOO GOOD TO BE TRUE

When someone is feeling out of control, experiencing intense worry, phobias, or panic attacks, coming to an understanding of the unconscious conflict that is at the source of their overwhelming emotion can provide almost immediate relief. Take the case of Aloha.

She had chronic pelvic pain that started when she was 11 but it escalated recently when she got married to her female partner whose children she was helping to raise. Aloha had great hope that there would be a surgical solution for her pelvic pain. She had had surgery to treat endometriosis, but though the surgery was successful she still had pain. Her doctors could not find the source of the pain so they referred her to me.

The first thing that comes to mind when considering pelvic pain is the possibility of sexual trauma in the individual's history. Sexual abuse often ends when girls turn eleven due to factors related to the child's maturation into adolescence, such as the abuser's fear of discovery or pregnancy, or issues of desire. The psychological pain of the sexual trauma can stem from a plethora of emotional conflicts. The fear of telling the truth and its impact can be primary. Will I be punished? Is it my fault? Will it ruin my mother's relationship? Will they believe me? Many complicated questions and no one to turn to. Maybe it's better to keep the secret. It's just easier to put it away; to get it "behind me." This is the perfect recipe for the fear and emotional pain to seek and find a physical expression. It isn't uncommon for children to develop pelvic pain in puberty following the experience of sexual abuse. Chronic migraines are often born within this scenario, and most likely supported by hormonal changes and menstruation. And with the onset of puberty and the physical changes of the body, deeper issues of sexual identity become very difficult to file away. Confusion, anxiety, fear and pain are inevitable under even unremarkable circumstances. With the experience of sexual trauma and the child's solitary misinterpretations and misunderstandings, the crisis gets much worse. The ability for a child to cope as he or she transitions to adolescence, limited as it is, inevitably fails when complicated by sexual abuse.

However, Aloha apparently did not fit this profile. She reported that she was not sexually abused. Her father was not in her life. Her mother was cold, distant, unemotional, and showed her no affection. I asked her how she felt about being touched. She said she was a "tomboy" as a child and there wasn't much touching growing up. She never liked the "girly" things. She didn't like playing with dolls. She met her first girlfriend in college. The relationship was difficult, filled with stress and what she defined as codependence. It lasted 10 years. Midway through that period her girlfriend was diagnosed with schizophrenia. Her emotional struggles were great and Aloha felt unable to "abandon" her until a point where it became unbearable and she then ended it.

She began a relationship with someone she found charming and attractive. Everything went well until it didn't. Her girlfriend stole Aloha's money, credit cards, and eventually her identity, so ending their five-year relationship.

In session she described her current partner as a wonderful person, emotionally stable and attractive. They have good communication, good sex, and they have similar interests and beliefs. She said she is high functioning, employed, contributes equally to what needs to be done, and co-parents with a minimum of conflict. But when the relationship started her pelvic pain got worse.

I want to mention why I am going into such detail about this case. I want to restate how important it is to listen to the whole story, to listen and observe carefully to what is being said and how it is being presented. We are not simply looking for symptoms to medicate but for the meaning behind the symptoms. There are many intelligent, thoughtful and well-intended psychiatrists who do what they feel is in the best interest of the patient by prescribing medication. But seeing the tip of the iceberg and attempting to smooth it over without concern for what lies beneath fails to take into consideration the most important part. I must emphasize the importance of learning the psychological causes of chronic pain if we are to help the patient get on the path to cure.

Modern bio-psychiatry attempts to make the tip of the iceberg disappear creating the illusion that the iceberg no longer exists. But of course it's just under the surface, and as the ship heads out to sea without benefit of the warning the ice had provided, there is high risk of a crash and a sinking. For this reason I feel that the impact of psychiatric medication may create the appearance of health but is ultimately counterproductive.

In my experience I have often seen patients' pelvic pain increase within an intimate and loving relationship. For example, if an individual has been a victim of sexual abuse at some point in their life, the experience of sex and its associations, even in a loving relationship, can be charged with complicated feelings potentially triggering pain, anxiety, depression or anger. If there is an unresolved self-blame complicating these emotions the sexual encounter can become an experience to avoid (or in some cases to reenact). If avoidance is the priority, a person may unconsciously seek a partner who is okay with that or who may be a nurturer or a "caretaker," someone whose self-worth is in some way tied to their ability to identify and care for the needs or pains of another. A person may use the pelvic pain to avoid sex. In an effort to hang on to the partner and not talk about sex (or abuse) directly, symptoms may develop, i.e.

pain or illness becomes the 'legitimate' reason one can't have sex. The partner doesn't want to worsen the pain or the condition so he or she backs off. An unspoken agreement is made. One's need for sex in the relationship is trumped by the other's experience of pain. And again, it's all unconscious.

But this typical scenario didn't seem to apply to Aloha's pelvic pain. There was no apparent sexual abuse and she reported a satisfying sex life. What could be the hidden psychological cause of the pain?

Aloha's two prior relationships had been with emotionally and financially draining partners. She had been attracted to both of them but both relationships turned out badly. Attraction in relationships is often the result of recognizing someone that wants or values what we believe we have to offer. And if this dynamic comes in combination with their expressing qualities of their own that we value based on our own sense of deficit, we've got a match. The cliché stating that opposites attract is based in this idea. If someone values our creativity, or intelligence, or extroversion, or for that matter our ability to clean up a mess, and these are the qualities that we feel defines us and supports our sense of self, we may be very drawn to this person. On the other hand, if we feel useless in some particular area and the other person expresses that quality with great competence, we may be drawn in their direction for that reason. If we feel we have very little to bring to the table, or in other words we suffer low self-worth, we may find ourselves attracted to those who are needy, or sick, or helpless, that is, someone we can at least take care of. We may as a result become drawn to partners who end up draining us emotionally or financially or both. What brought the relationship together in the first place may become the point of conflict that tears it apart.

Aloha had not had a strong bond with either mother or father, and now for the first time she found herself with someone who was strong and supportive, a "wonderful" person, as she put it. You would think the response would be "Finally! At last! Everything is awesome now!" But the expectation that she will be hurt nonetheless found a home long time ago, and was internalized after years of neglect and pain. She's now forty, she's found somebody she loves, but she'd better not let her guard down. Just in case.

"Maybe things are too good to be true," says the unconscious inner voice.

Maybe she's afraid that she's sliding into a situation where she will give everything and get nothing or worse in return.

"The passion, the excitement, will betray me in the end," she thinks. "I must tone it down to protect myself."

So how does she protect herself? How does she slow the passion down so the inevitable doesn't happen one more time?

The voice continues, "Don't let your guard down. You could be hurt. Things may be worse than they seem. She could have an affair. She could leave suddenly realizing you have nothing she needs. Don't let your guard down."

And her body responds, and symptoms develop. The body tenses and tightens down and then it just hurts. Real pain, in the body, delivered on demand. The bodymind doing what it does, responding to the cry for help. "I'm going to be hurt, please help me." So it does.

And the lifelong pattern based on the internalizations of childhood continues to run her life. But it is time to take the power back. Time to give the little girl a break. Give her a hug, thank her for doing her best and reinterpreting where she's been and what it means.

This analysis came to me toward the end of the session. It felt right based on all I heard and felt in the room. She was afraid of moving too fast and of loving too much. The desire was so strong and she wanted it so badly. But the voice was telling her to slow down. If she crashes this time she may not recover. Slow down. Tighten up. Protect yourself. And the pelvic pain did just that. It slowed everything down. And it required constant attention.

The interpretation seemed to connect immediately. She was ready to understand.

"Of course," she said. "It makes so much sense. I think you hit it."

Her body seemed to release as she continued.

"I'm afraid she's going to leave. Even though everything is great, I just don't trust. I expect the worst. And the pain is somehow easier to deal with than the fear."

Once this unconscious fear came to light, the work was able to focus more directly on the voice inside that has been running the show and provoking what she fears most for a long time. Finding ways to take the power back. Becoming aware of the old automatic patterns of response based in the interpretations and expectations of an abused child. We talked about taking the risk of trusting and growing in awareness, and the experience of managing the old fear, giving it more direct expression and in so doing, preventing its unconscious expression in pelvic pain. Over time Aloha's pain disappeared completely and she began to allow herself to fully enjoy her family.

Helping my patients take the risk of understanding their stories makes me feel grateful. They usually find their way into my office at that moment when they have had enough. They are ready to take the required journey, to take the risk of understanding where they have come from and who they are. I have tremendous admiration for the people who have been through so much and are able to get on the path to cure, which requires the courage to feel the feelings and look closely at what hurts so much.

8

Why Now?

"The patient is hardly ever conscious of the significance of the date, but with exploration, it turns out to be the anniversary of a loss or a traumatic event, as if physical symptoms were commemorating that event in the place of conscious memories."

Darian Leader, Psychoanalyst

THE ANNIVERSARY "COINCIDENCE" AS A

PSYCHOLOGICAL PHENOMENON

It is commonplace to consider the "when" associated with the onset of pain as a potentially meaningful variable. The question, "When did you begin to feel the pain?" is asked automatically in any treatment setting. Physicians, therapists, nurses and intake personnel will routinely ask this question, and yet in most instances there is an incomplete understanding of how important this simple piece of information can be in understanding and resolving chronic pain. Most often it is asked with the goal of understanding what a patient might have been doing physically just prior to the onset of pain. Was there an impact? An exertion? Did the patient eat or ingest something toxic? It is rare outside of a psychologist's office to hear the question asked with reference to past events or possibly a current milestone such as a birthday that may relate to a significant past event. The unconscious is remarkable in its ability to remember the precise moment of a significant loss or trauma in one's history and to remind us that its anniversary is coming or has arrived. The gorilla will leave tracks that can be followed right to the emotional source of the pain.

"The pain started right before my birthday. It was my fifty-fourth birthday," she said.

"Does anything come to mind that is significant about the fact of your fifty-fourth birthday?" I asked.

She thought for a moment, "My mom got cancer when she was 54. I guess I forgot."

But of course she didn't forget. And her body reminded her loudly and clearly. I can't count the number of times patients have realized over time or told me outright that their pain started around the anniversary (often on the day) of a parent's death or onset of illness at the patient's current age. The anniversary can trigger an unconscious memory of the unresolved emotion such as grief, guilt or anxiety associated with the loss that is expressed in physical pain or illness. These synchronicities of timing are most often interpreted as simple coincidence and not given more than a passing thought. But this is a mistake. It is precisely these unconscious connections that need to be drawn out of the gorilla's realm and into the light of conscious awareness. And this unconscious connection is often one of the first that patients understand almost immediately once given "permission" to go there. They very often know the truth of this connection intuitively but need credible confirmation to help them bring it to light.

ARTHUR

It has been my observation that lower back pain is often a physical expression of two specific emotions that have gone underground, feeling unsupported (unloved) and/or carrying unresolved grief. I see this particular adaptation of the unconscious over and over.

Take Arthur, for example. He was a 36-year-old man who came to see me one day late in the fall. His back had been hurting since the previous December. He had injured himself on the job at a waste treatment plant during some minor physical activity. His initial physician had ordered an MRI. Although the test revealed nothing, Arthur was prescribed a narcotic pain medication for short-term use. With the side effects of the medication becoming more uncomfortable and the relief provided minimal he returned to his doctor who then referred Arthur to my office.

"I don't know why I'm here. The pain is real. Believe me, it's not in my head." I reassured him he didn't need to convince me. I told him I knew the pain was very real. I started with a detailed history as with every patient.

"When did the pain start?" I asked.

"Last December, I twisted it on the job," he said. "I remember it very well because it happened almost exactly a year after my father died."

"Your father died? That must have been difficult."

"Not difficult at all," he said with disdain. "I didn't go to the funeral. He was a bastard."

I recognize the tension in his tone and I saw the pain in his eyes. We were entering well-traveled territory. It's uncanny how frequently I see people who have injured themselves or taken ill near the anniversary of a parent's death. It is important to them to feel it is "no big deal," but unfortunately it is often a big deal, a big unresolved deal with many painful emotions vying for expression.

I continue to listen. The more he talks the more I will hear and understand, and the better I will be able to help him resolve the issues that are causing pain.

"He was a terrible father, the worst," he continued. "I can't even call him a father. He was always gone and when he did come around, he would scream at us and hit us."

As we met over the weeks our therapeutic relationship strengthened. It was clear he enjoyed the connection and the ability to share his story and express what he was feeling. He was easy going and liked to joke around. But it was as though he needed to communicate to me (and to himself) that he was fine, "no problems here." Aware of his fear of exposing his vulnerability too quickly, I talked to him about the mind. I made reference to the iceberg analogy, only the smallest amount of ice showing and most of it hidden.

"The biggest part of our mind is unconscious to us," I said. "Hidden from view but still working hard and in many ways running our life."

I felt he was ready to go deeper, to explore the complicated feelings.

"Did you ever think your father was capable of change?" I asked him.

"Maybe, when I was a kid," he said. "But I realized after a while that he wouldn't. He was just a son-of-a-bitch and that was that."

"What was it like growing up with your father?" I asked.

Softening a bit he told me that when he as a kid he used to fantasize that his father would change. He saw a family on television with a loving father and he wanted that father to be his father. He said he wanted his father to apologize and tell him he loved him and was proud of him. He said he needed to know his father loved him. He said he needed that from his father more than anything. He needed a father that made him feel safe and loved.

"But I didn't get it," he said. "And it made me feel alone and angry."

As children we need to bond with our mother and father and to feel loved and appreciated by them. We need the world to be a loving world, one that values who we are. And our mother and father happen to be the world that we see and experience. Our beliefs about the world are established by the treatment we receive from mom and dad. Is the world a safe place? A loving place? Can we expect to be accepted or rejected? If those whose most important job is to love us fail to do so, why would we expect anyone else to care about what we need? And maybe we interpret this treatment as being our fault, that we don't really deserve love. So the child grows up and the part of the iceberg that sticks out of the water, his conscious mind, develops based on the experience of the previous years. His experience teaches him the world does not care and will not change despite the need and the wish. The part under water, the unconscious, interprets this experience as best it can for its age. And the unconscious interpretation creates a feeling of being unsafe, alone, unloved, and is often accompanied by an unhealthy dose of self-blame, and this is what complicates the whole picture. And creates pain.

As children, when we don't get what we need, when we don't feel loved, we assume unconsciously it is our fault. We see and feel the disappointment day in and day out. We long for the love and it just doesn't come. And very often we don't know the world is or should be any different. We only know what we experience and feel. We know where the failure lies, but we nonetheless blame ourselves, and this is a scenario guaranteed to complicate the emotion and create pain. But we hang on to the wish of redemption, "I will finally be loved one day." We do everything we can to elicit that love and we hang on to the wish but it just doesn't come. And then dad dies and with it the wish. And what rises up is not redemption, but pain. Anger, grief and pain. Lots and lots of pain.

Once the support that the wish may have provided is gone it often gets expressed through the body. Low back pain, fatigue, irritability is often the result. And when the anniversary of dad's death comes around, the patient bends funny or lifts something heavy and boom, the back is out and chronic pain sets in and becomes the unconscious expression of anger, grief and self-blame.

Arthur had been running on anger the whole year after his father died. First comes, "I'm glad he's gone. He was a bad father. He gave me nothing. I will get back at him by ignoring his death like he ignored me." But after a while the revenge doesn't help. His father is

91

gone. His father never gave him what he needed and there is an emotional impact. And this impact must be felt and understood before it will be relieved. His father isn't coming back and there is an emotional price to pay, and the revenge fantasy has failed to defeat the feelings. Depression sets in and then injury. The unconscious continues to express what is real. It is now time for Arthur to take the power back and feel what needs to be felt, and finally understand and accept this piece of his story.

As Arthur began to accept and eventually understand what was happening, the pain eased and then shortly thereafter was gone. He accepted and expressed the grief of not having the father he needed and with his death, would never have.

Hundreds of variations on the Arthur story have presented themselves in my office over the years. Lower back pain, fatigue and depression are symptoms that often present themselves on the anniversary of a parent's death. In some cases, the parent may not have been abusive but the feelings of grief possibly complicated by guilt or anger over the loss of emotional support were never felt and understood fully enough to be resolved, and the pain remained to be expressed through the body. Pain is pain. If it's there and it's strong enough and we refuse to look at it or feel it consciously, our body will take over. Until we look at it, feel it, and understand its source, it will be expressed one way or another.

One final thought on Arthur's case. I had mentioned that when Arthur came in the first time he told me that he had gotten a prescription for a narcotic pain medication from his PCP but that it was no longer working to relieve the pain. The thing about narcotics is that they not only have the ability in many cases to manage physical pain (at least for a while), but they can also numb emotional pain (at least for a while). But as Arthur, and all my patients who have gone this route learn, the relief is temporary and when the pain comes back it can be worse than ever.

In order to be resolved, and by that I mean cured, the pain as communication must be listened to. As Dr. Freud tells us, we can't run away from ourselves. Numbing the pain may provide temporary relief but until it is understood, until our story is understood, it hasn't gone anywhere.

CHARLIE

The workings of the unconscious can seem rather amazing, as in its efforts to heal both body and mind. Here, for example is the remarkable case of a 42-year-old tree doctor named Charlie.

He had injured his left leg on the job falling from a roof. He shared, as it turned out, that his father had also injured himself at the age of 42, falling from a fence, also the left leg. His father's wound became seriously infected, wasn't properly treated and gangrene developed. When Charlie was 17 his father had his leg amputated and was forced to stop working. Five years later when Charlie was 22 his father died. Due to family hardship Charlie chose to quit school and go to work to support the family.

Now, at the age of his father's injury, he was suffering the same kind of pain his father did having had a similar accident. A painful reunion with his father one might say. Sounds crazy, like a freak accident. However, these "coincidences" might be hard for me to believe if they didn't walk, or should I say, limp into my office over and over and over again.

As we explored in chapter two, another reason Charlie's story seems unlikely is because the role of the unconscious most often falls outside the competency or financial interest of most physicians. In this 21st century culture that relies on technology and most recently, looks to neuroscience to solve all of our ills, the unconscious is ignored. We understand technology and the body's organs far better than we understand the mind. A picture of the brain can reveal many interesting things and make for many interesting TED Talks, but one critical discovery it will never make is the working and function of the unconscious. And although neuroscience minimizes the significance of the mind's elusive nature, it remains that an understanding of the mind is vital to the healing of human beings.

TESS

Unresolved grief can lay dormant in the unconscious for a lifetime and then come knocking years and years later. One of the doctors I work with called me about Tess. "Could you see her? She's crying. She can't handle her pain."

She comes in to the office. A brilliant 85-year-old woman. Good sense of humor. Twenty years of chronic back pain but just recently she started crying.

"I can't take the pain anymore. I've had enough. It's just overwhelming," she said.

Her daughters, one of whom lives with her, are worried about her and tell me she is depressed because of the pain. We discuss her history. Tess's mother had an "anxiety disorder," was nervous about everything. She died at 85. Tess is 85. Suddenly overcome with depression due to pain. I said it was interesting that for 20 years she coped well with back pain but now (just shortly after her birthday) it becomes unbearable and accompanied by depression. I suggested we talk about mom.

SAM

Sam came in one day. He has an excellent job. Manager at an amusement park with 100 employees. Fun job. Great job. Great marriage. Takes good care of himself. Suddenly he has groin pain. He's wants a stimulator, an electrical device that's implanted in the spine to reduce pain. He's referred to me for a psychological evaluation.

"When did the pain start?"

"Last year."

"Tell me about your childhood."

I learn his dad had MS. He was wheelchair bound with no bladder or bowel control. He was put in the VA Hospital because the family couldn't take care of him with all the kids at home. Dad was miserable. He hated it there and it made the family miserable. He wanted to come home but they couldn't take care of him. Mom couldn't raise the kids and take care of dad so he stayed in the hospital and he died at 48. How old is Sam? 48.

GEORGE

George came to me with shoulder pain that had led to migraines. I asked him when the pain began.

"About five years ago."

"What were you doing?"

"I was lifting my wife. We were snowmobiling and playing around in the snow. She fell and I picked her up. I was showing off and lifted her up to my shoulders."

This was a man in his forties. It seemed somewhat unusual to me that he had lifted his wife onto his shoulders. I asked him about it.

"Well," he said. "This was he anniversary of my father's death and I was trying to cheer myself up."

"When did your father die?" I asked.

"I was a kid. He was only forty-four."

"How old were you when you were snowmobiling?"

"It was five years ago and I'm forty-nine now so I was…"

"Forty-four like your dad when he died," I said.

"I guess so," said George.

How did the father die? Suicide. How did he kill himself? He put a shotgun in his mouth and the shot went right through his skull and now George has chronic headaches. George was never given any counseling as a kid and until now had never sought any psychological treatment.

He went on to describe his mother's reaction to the death of dad.

"She just fell apart. And she's been an emotional wreck my whole life. I've had to take care of her, to support her," he said.

She was an emotional wreck. He had to be his mother's mother. And how did the pain cycle begin? Supporting his wife.

These symbolic connections occur over and over again with hundreds, actually thousands of patients. I get that it is hard to understand how the unconscious works in this way, but the evidence is clear. Anniversaries can trigger memories both conscious and unconscious, and unresolved emotion that has been defended against for a lifetime can trigger a pain, an illness or an accident as it pushes to the surface to make itself known. As I have said before it is often somehow perceived as easier to manage a physical pain than to have to relive the trauma of loss still defined unconsciously as unmanageable or even unbearable. But once the connection is made and it enters conscious awareness, diffusion of the painful emotion begins.

It often occurs that patients who injure themselves around the time of their parent's death have not fully resolved or at least fully experienced their grief. If the loss is experienced as a child and the child isn't helped to understand what is happening and to feel the feelings, it will remain hidden and unresolved. I will occasionally hear the story from an adult that when their mother or dad or sister or brother died they were not given any help in understanding what was actually happening. The traumatic "disappearance" remains unresolved as "no one was allowed to talk about it."

Experiencing the loss as an adult may lead to a need to be "strong," for a variety of reasons. Being the oldest sibling or the one that "takes care of everyone and everything" just wouldn't allow for grieving with the belief that one can "cry later when there isn't so much to do." But that time never really comes. And the pain will find an alternative path to express itself, if not now then later, and very often an anniversary provides the perfect opportunity to see the connection, revisit the grief and hopefully end the chronic pain.

IT'S A GUY THING

Another important reality I confront each day is the "lack of interest" in therapy by many men. The resistance to talking about one's experience (read: feelings) is often based in the anxiety triggered by a threat of losing control. Talking about and seeking treatment for physical injuries is perceived as being a lot easier than exploring old unresolved emotion that can leave one feeling confused or vulnerable, and requires one to surrender a certain degree of control.

I see many chronic pain patients who have sustained work injuries in very demanding factory jobs. Working at a repetitive, physically challenging job for a long period of time is a high-risk scenario for back injury.

I feel compassion for the men who lose their ability to work due to injury on the job. The job a person has been performing for a number of years is a significant, if not the most important factor in supporting that person's sense of who they are. This sense of identity is not necessarily defined by the actual nuts and bolts of the job but more likely by what it may mean to the person, for example being useful or being a provider or simply being competent with managing one's life. In addition, the relationships established on the job and often taken for granted can become a source of great pain when lost along with the job. Part of this pain involves a feeling of being useless and alone and often results in an experience of great vulnerability.

Whether the onslaught of painful feeling is triggered by the loss of a job or the loss of a loved one does not matter. Defending against the vulnerability becomes priority number one for many men. Remaining "strong" in the face of this pain is the goal. When explored in therapy, this experience often translates into a confrontation with a feeling of profound "weakness". And if the man grew up in an environment as a child and adolescent that did not tolerate feelings of any kind, much less weakness, this feeling can be unbearable.

For many men, to enter therapy is to admit they are unable to defend themselves against the vulnerability, and it leaves them feeling overpowered. In many cases, there is a belief that the physical pain is easier to manage than talking about their feeling of weakness. We all deserve to be able to defend ourselves against the pain in whatever manner we choose, but unfortunately avoiding an exploration of our emotions because we fear they will defeat us, leaves us weaker not stronger, and in pain.

JACK

Jack was referred to my office for a surgery evaluation.

"I don't think psychology is helpful," he told me. "I had a strong role model as a father. We went hunting and fishing together. He was a great man and a great father. I had no problems as a child. Occasionally I was disciplined but it was my fault for not listening or being lazy…or crying. He hated it when I cried."

"When did your pain start?" I asked.

"My back went out in 1995."

"When did your father die?"

"1995."

"What was the most difficult thing you've had to experience?"

"Losing my father."

Experiencing the grief that comes with the loss of a significant person in our life as important as a father or mother often involves coming to terms with conflicted feelings toward that person. In exploring Jack's relationship to his father it became clear that there were feelings he was carrying that somehow undermined the need to idealize his father. His father would not tolerate Jack's sadness as a child. Crying was not an option. As a result Jack would feel he was a disappointment to his father whenever he was sad. This feeling that he was somehow disappointing his father complicated the grief he felt when his father died. Coming to terms with this unconscious experience in therapy enabled Jack to understand this painful aspect of his inner life. Over the course of the work we did together he was also able to access some anger toward his father for, in effect, punishing him for having the normal feelings of a child. In feeling the feelings, Jack came to understand, accept and no longer be threatened by this conflict he had been carrying unconsciously for so long.

Men like Jack are often more open to addressing their pain through surgery or other medical treatments than looking at feelings. Surgeries become war wounds received in the warrior's battle against the external enemy called pain. Unfortunately, the source of the pain may not be the physical injury but something lying deeper within, and with every unnecessary surgery the pain just gets worse.

NORBERT

As a project manager for a large construction company, it became more and more difficult for Norbert to do his job due to overwhelming back pain until finally he could no longer go in at all. The referring pain doctor told me there were minimal findings on the MRI. His wife would drive him to my office in their minivan. He would lie on a mattress on the floor of the minivan for the drive. In the office he could hold himself up for only a few minutes due to severe mid back pain.

In session, I learned that Norbert grew up in Cleveland. He shared that his father was very strict and "expected perfection." There was no margin for error whether in school or with chores at home. He was required to cut the grass in a crisscross pattern, first north south, then east west, creating a perfectly square checkerboard pattern, not too short, not too tall. If his father was displeased, which was often the case, he would come up behind his son and smack him hard on the back and correct his imperfect performance. With the sound of the mower and his father's preferred sneak attack approach, he never knew when he would get smacked on the back. His father would also surprise him with a smack to the back as he studied at his desk facing the wall of his bedroom. The smacks were often accompanied by an angry and aggressive tongue-lashing for some perceived imperfect performance by Norbert.

"You idiot! I told you NOT to come in until you finished in the garage. You don't move on to a new job until the first one is finished!"

So okay, mid-back, right. But why now? Why at this moment of his life?

As he continues to tell his story I learn that earlier in the year his boss of many years with whom he worked well lost his job and was replaced by a new manager to oversee all projects. Norbert reported that the new manager seemed to be very stressed at all times. One day shortly after meeting the new manager his first week on the job, Norbert was shaken as the manager burst into the office screaming at him about the delay in the plans he had promised to deliver at a certain time. Norbert reported he actually made no such promise. After delivering the plans there was another sudden surprise explosion about mistakes that were made. Threats of incompetence and name-calling of other kinds would follow and things went downhill from there. Norbert was unable to please the manager and with his growing anxiety finally came a back spasm that sent him to the floor.

I began to make the obvious connection between his experience of anxiety with his father and that with the manager. The feeling of never being safe, and despite best efforts a feeling of never being good enough creating a debilitating anxiety that now was being expressed in his back. The unconscious expectation of a surprise smack to the back became exactly that. He got it. There was no doubt. This was an easy one to understand. The more he talked and expressed his experience of anxiety and anger in words, the more relief he felt.

However when we began to talk about his returning to work the pain returned. We explored what changes could be made to help him feel safer and less vulnerable to the outbursts of his manager. I sent a note to his employer releasing him to return to work with certain conditions requested. Regular meetings would be held at the beginning of each week to establish specific expectations with scheduled follow up reviews. Random interference would be kept to a minimum.

I suggested to Norbert that he pull his desk away from the wall and turn it around to face the door. He smiled and agreed that was a good idea. He returned to work the next week.

9

Chronic Pain Triggers

I AM NOT MY MOTHER

Suffering emotional deprivation in childhood or some other experience of trauma at the hand of a parent at a time when there are no inner or outer resources to help understand or to cope, can create an overpowering and confusing experience of emotion, as well as internalizations of the self-blaming sort. Memory and awareness of this experience often leads to, among other conscious and unconscious responses, a promise to oneself to never be like that parent. Being able to feel and understand the emotion, and by that I mean knowing better where it came from, can help one recognize when it is being expressed "in the wrong direction." Being able to know the appropriate target of your anger, whether expressed directly or not, can prevent collateral damage to the relationships you value. Although our closest relationships can often trigger the emotion, they are usually not the cause of the primal wound that continues to run your life and express itself in chronic pain. Owning the emotion and knowing where it came from is a first step to healing. To never repeat the pattern of abuse with one's own children becomes a promise to oneself. But of course, it's a complicated emotional business.

A patient I saw recently came in complaining of severe

headaches. She reported having been abandoned emotionally by her mother, describing the experience of being denied affection of any kind. She said her mother was diagnosed as bipolar and was addicted to pain medication. Her father and stepmother raised her.

The patient got pregnant and had a daughter at a young age and made the promise to herself that she would never be like her mother. She would never be angry, and absolutely never abandon her daughter in any way. She created this promise as an expression of her pain and anger, and unknown to her to manage the unconscious self-blame based in rejection by her mother. This pact she made with herself resulted in a very charged emotional state tied to being a loving mother. She would never be angry, never have mood swings, and never abandon her child. She would provide love and nourishment and be responsive to her daughter's needs. But there was just one problem. Her own life had been devoid of this experience. She'd never been on the receiving end of this quality of parenting and her understanding of the range of her own emotions was underdeveloped as a result. It's like making a commitment to driving someone 100 miles with only enough gas to go 25. You will end up on the side of the road needing someone's help, reinforcing the self-blame. Motherhood creates unforeseen demands on even the most emotionally prepared mothers. Being able to draw on one's own experience of having had "good enough" parents is helpful but not always enough. If you did not have this experience and never learned to understand or at least tolerate strong feelings, then motherhood will indeed be a challenging experience. The next frustration or demand is always standing by to undermine the best of parenting intentions. When the child will not sleep, will not eat, or will not stop crying there will likely be exasperation on the part of a parent. And maybe some anger. Actually there might be quite a bit of anger, and maybe a feeling of being trapped, and a desire to run and escape.

Now having these feelings may not quite satisfy the established terms of the good mother contract. In other words, simply experiencing the intense feelings triggered by the demands of motherhood create a sense of failing. Never learning how to cope with such feelings based in the deprivations of her own childhood leaves her ill equipped to get through the feelings. She has already judged herself a failure and is feeling hopeless. The unconscious creation of pain or illness or a slip into post partum depression may be the only justifiable out. She may be feeling profoundly overwrought emotionally, profoundly depressed and finding it nearly impossible to be there for her child. And this produces a confrontation with a betrayal of the commitment she made to her daughter, i.e. not to be her own mother. But she has failed, and forgiving herself will require her to forgive her mother, and this is too great a conflict to contain. Debilitating headaches and a feeling of hopelessness are the result.

Joy, anger, guilt, grief. We experience a wide range of emotions and based on the quality of our own understanding and the interpretation we bring to each feeling will render the experience as tolerable or not. If certain feelings are interpreted as too destructive or hateful, negative self-judgment will result and an emotional conflict will leave us feeling more and more miserable.

Finding yourself in the position as a new mother of caring for a child who seems uncomfortable, struggling to sleep, keeping you awake for hours upon hours, results in a very normal experience of all sorts of feelings, some "acceptable" and some not. If the mother had a loving parent and the parent was comfortable with all the feelings that came up and was dedicated to the child, then the mother will more likely be in a better position to acknowledge the feelings and know they will pass.

But if a patient had a mother who disappeared or was unresponsive to needs, that patient may experience a sense of terror or panic, anger and shame when confronted by her own normal feelings. The preconscious conflict that arises in sensing she has failed to not be her mother creates chaos in the system.

Drawing attention to this in therapy often gets a resounding affirmative response. As though the conflict is very near the surface just needing an empathic acknowledgement.

"Sounds like your mother," I say. "Did you make a promise to not be your mother?"

"Yes! The day I got pregnant."

Which leads into an exploration of feelings, maybe feelings of wanting to run or escape, maybe even feelings of wanting to hurt the child. And I point out two important things. First, feelings are not behaviors. Feeling you want to run away is not the same as running away. Second, you are human and these feelings are normal and very common. If you feel ashamed that you feel this way or you hate yourself for having these feelings and you are afraid that you might act on them, then you are attempting to deny being a human being and it simply makes the situation worse. You can't deny feelings. And the interpretation that you are your mother because you are having particular feelings is flawed. You are having feelings as your mother had feelings because you are both human. And humans respond to feelings in different ways. You didn't commit yourself to not having feelings; you committed yourself to not abandoning your child. These are two very different things.

Anger and frustration are real. It is important to acknowledge your anger and frustration as real and valid. Having these feelings does not mean you are a bad mother. Having these feelings does not mean you have betrayed your commitment to "not be your mother."

The exploration in therapy can take time. It is a process that requires care and commitment of its own. As patients come to understand the nature of the conflict, there can be an immediate feeling of relief supported by an understanding and empathic response. There is a reaching out. They want to reconcile the need to run with the need to not be their mother, to break the cycle of neglect. But not having been given the nurturance they needed as a child has resulted in fearing and resisting the responsibilities that have confronted them throughout their lives and now of motherhood. They don't know how to be an adult. They don't know how to be responsible. And then they are given a child.

Therapy helps them find compassion for themselves and leads them to take their own first steps toward an understanding and an acceptance of their feelings. Where feelings always resulted in an automatic and involuntary behavioral response, the feelings can now be experienced, and a choice can be made as to how exactly to respond. Taking the power back involves experiencing the feeling, and with awareness and understanding, stepping back from the automatic unconscious response. We can't expect to not have feelings but we can bring greater resources to managing them, and in time we will feel the diffusion of their painful intensity.

LOSS AND (SOMETIMES) FREEDOM

I'll bet you've heard of a couple where the husband dies and very shortly thereafter the wife dies. Or vice versa. Sometimes the second death is a year later, sometimes just a few months, and often, weeks or even just days later. We can ask ourselves why this happens. Certainly the answer lies somewhere in the power of our minds.

If the husband dies and the wife feels an emotional emptiness and a level of grief leaving her feeling that life is no longer worth living, the mind can begin to shut down the body. That is how powerful the mind can be and how it can control bodily processes.

I've also seen the reverse where a wife was in a difficult marriage for many years; the husband passes away and the children tell me their mother has come alive as a result. She has more energy for life than they have ever seen, she's taking classes, traveling, volunteering. And she looks better and more healthy than she has for years.

If negative psychosocial stressors are not addressed the mind can be destructive to the body and if these stressors are removed the mind can uplift the body. Psychological stressors can also be addressed and resolved through therapy. Through an understanding of their impact choices can be made to create change through communication, boundary setting, or outright detachment from the stress causing entity.

SAYING IT -
THE HEALING POWER OF EXPRESSION

A year ago a couple came to see me. The husband had been suffering severe migraines. He told me headaches had been a problem his whole life but they'd gotten worse in the last few years and he was ready to do something about it. His history revealed that "all his life" actually meant all his adult life; he hadn't had headaches as a child.

He had served in World War II during the Ardennes Offensive; better known as the Battle of the Bulge. His wife and I listened as he shared his experience of having to lie in a bunker for three days with continuous bombing all around him. By continuous he really meant non-stop bombing 'every few seconds' for three days.

"Boom, boom, boom!" He gestured as he spoke showing us how the bombs were falling.

"You didn't know if you'd be dead in the next second, or maimed. No eating, no sleeping for three days," he said.

It was hard for me to imagine what that must have been like. I said, "If that was me, it would have driven me crazy."

He broke into tears. "It did," he said. "There hasn't been a day I haven't thought of it."

His wife spoke for the first time. "You never even talked about it."

"No," he said. "I didn't."

We sat silently for a while. There is really nothing to be said thinking about the pain some people carry for a lifetime.

110

AWAKENING TO SELF-WORTH – STOPPING THE ABUSE

She never knew her biological father. She had an adoptive father but he clearly preferred his biological children and was never loving or affectionate to her. As an adult she found herself in relationships with men who treated her badly, who also didn't show her any love. She was playing out the unconscious drive to get it right this time, to mend the bond that never happened when she was a child. Like taking a test over or redoing a class at school. The unconscious belief goes something like this, "If I'm nice enough to him, he'll love me this time." To do that, to make the correction, she would need to find a "worthy opponent," someone not very generous in the loving department. This is an essential part of the drama. The reenactment is abusive but familiar. And if the love isn't forthcoming this time, well continuing to play the victim role can at least lighten the painful load of self-blame and guilt.

Her live-in boyfriend had the necessary requirement. He was distant and often insulting. He grew up in chaotic conditions, and had been basically neglected and emotionally abandoned. He was terrified that she would leave him but it wasn't something he would tell her or even admit to himself. He just knew that he liked to have her under his control. He noticed that if he was distant, she would try even harder to be loving to him, so he played her like a game. If he wanted sex he would behave decently or treat her with a little humor or niceness every couple weeks.

This particular story with this particular patient did have a happy ending (for half of the couple anyway.) At around age forty the woman, responsible and dependable at her job, a job that meant a lot to her, began to break down emotionally. She was exhausted and could hardly function. She saw the pattern in her relationship that she was unable to get free of throughout her adult life, and she was burned out and wanted help.

An early experience of love and nurturance gives you the energy and confidence to move through life. But if you don't get what you need as a child, it will play out in your life. We try to satisfy the need in relationship after relationship but without the necessary inner resources, we provoke the same dynamic as we play the same role.

She came in for help and she worked hard to understand her experience and why it continued to play out. She found the courage to look closely at the emotional pain she had been in for so long, and although it often seemed too painful to continue, she went on, she learned and she created change in her life. She now maintains awareness of her old tendency to be drawn to the emotionally broken and creates a disciplined boundary refusing to step into the old drama. She knows she deserves better and that this effort will be required for her to get there.

10

Lifecycles

"Family life may not have prepared him for school life...he may
still rather be the baby at home than the big child at school..."
from Identity and the Life Cycle, 1959
Erik H. Erikson, Psychologist

The above quote describes a familiar situation to many of us with
children. The reality of human growth and experience suggests,
however, that tough transitions are not just for kids, and not based on
simply wanting to "stay home." The unconscious complications,
doubts and anxieties that can accompany transitions throughout life
can challenge our sense of wellbeing and health. Whether the life
phase is infancy to childhood or maturity to retirement, what we
often look forward to with confidence and excitement, can suddenly
confront us with an experience of personal vulnerability and loss.

The experience of lifecycle transition continues throughout our
lives. Just when we feel we have it figured out (or not), life demands
we step into a new role. We must move from birth through
childhood and school, to work and family, to retirement and
preparation for the end of life. If supports have been in place and
competencies have been attained, chances are we find a way to
accommodate or even celebrate life change. Our family and our

culture prepare us for some of the well-traveled transitions. Certain milestones such as graduation and marriage are reinforced by ritual, allowing us to anticipate the next growth stage in advance, providing an opportunity to participate and find a degree of control as we take each new step.

Some transitions, however, do not give us much time, or give us the means to prepare. Or, circumstances have left us unprepared. How does one plan for the end of life, not having a clue when that might be? How does one prepare for the inevitable separation that some transitions require? The uncertainty of not knowing where we are, or how a life change and its impact will unfold, or how it will affect those we love, can create a need to unconsciously "take control," often prematurely interrupting or terminating a natural process.

The following case examples explore potentially positive life transitions that were interrupted by somatic expressions of anxiety and pain. Transitional disruptions such as these are typically accompanied by unconscious "solutions" based in a regression to the perceived safety of what came before, often justified by illness, injury or the emergence of chronic symptoms. These regressions serve to relieve the individual of the anxiety, guilt, isolation, despair, or identity disorientation, associated with the transitional requirement to take on a new role or identity.

RETIREMENT – LOSING CONNECTION

A phenomenon I often see in my practice involves the link between a patient's chronic pain and an acute feeling of their disconnection from life. Relationships, activities, interests, jobs, pleasures, efforts of all kinds have broken down and the rebuilding process, if attempted, has failed to gain momentum. Chronic pain or various symptoms develop, often accompanied by depression or a general malaise. Sometimes it is a lifelong battle based in trauma, abuse, injury, disease, and loss. And sometimes it can sneak up on us when we least expect it. Retirement can be one of these situations.

I began work with a 66-year-old patient who had come down with a 104-degree fever two months after retiring from a very successful career as a business executive. The job had required a vigilance of attention to the sales performance of dozens of employees. There was rarely any down time, which is the way he liked it, always something to attend to. Prior to being referred to my office he had been to Mayo Clinic and Mass General Hospital seeking diagnosis and treatment. A full workup at each of the medical facilities revealed nothing that could explain the symptom. Ibuprofen would reduce the fever for only an hour or two. He was burning up and no one knew why. He was told that medical science could not help him. It was predicted that if the fever continued as it was, he could die within six months.

In our early therapeutic work together it was quickly revealed that his sense of self-worth was supported by one thing only, and that was his job and the experience of staying busy. His sense of personal value, identity, and connection to life were all based in his going to work and in the very demanding role he fulfilled. The decision to retire was motivated by certain inner and outer pressures, such as age and money in the bank, as well as the culturally indoctrinated belief that one should want to retire more than anything else.

Unfortunately, the power of the job to actually keep him healthy emotionally (and physically) was overlooked. The confrontation with stillness that he experienced in retirement created anxiety and disorientation, and this step into the unknown, for which he was unprepared had "overheated" his mind.

If there is only one element in our life from which we draw sustenance, meaning, or personal value, and this one element is lost, we may be at risk of great difficulty. Interestingly, we are often unaware of the power this one connection has in our life to keep us okay. The impact of losing this "handle" to the world can take us by surprise. The development of inner resources, based in connection to work, relationships, activities, interests, spiritual connections, pleasures of all kinds, and often stillness, can sustain us at a time of loss. The world provides an infinite variety of stimuli to which we can develop an interest or connection. We only need a few to help us feel alive, and support us in those times of loss or disconnection that are inevitable in a human life. If all the power is given to only one element in our life, we are setting ourselves up for a loss from which we may not recover.

My patient was fortunate that a return to part-time work was available to him, and in giving himself permission to return, his temperature returned to normal, the fire finally went out.

Our therapeutic work continues and is focused on an understanding of the anxiety accompanying his experience of stillness, the development of other critical connections, and on a deeper reflection of the transition to retirement including the associated meaning and impact on his sense of identity.

ENGULFED BY LOVE AND SUPPORT

She was a star softball player from a young age. She enjoyed the support of her family, whose weekends and often weeks were dedicated to traveling from game to game. The activity of coming together to celebrate her success served to define the family's life and defuse the anxiety so familiar to her at a younger age. As she moved through adolescence, when the challenge of coming to a healthy sense of identity can provide relentless difficulty and confusion, she found herself on the receiving end of validation from her family and from the community, both peers and adults. But something wasn't quite right.

Toward the end of her final year of high school, as she attempted to assess the desirability of a number of college offers, she was experiencing inner doubts as to what she really wanted, and feeling external pressure to choose one scholarship or another. A heightened anxiety overtook her as graduation approached, and she became aware of her parents' own growing agitation coming from what she interpreted as her indecision. As she began to seriously consider taking a year off to relieve the growing pressure, she received a final offer from UCLA, representing the most valuable scholarship from the best school. She accepted the offer. With her parents' renewed exuberance and support, preparations began for her move to Los Angeles. She was to join the Bruins, one of the great teams in college sports. That summer, however, a hiking accident left her with a broken ankle. She was referred to my office when after nearly a year of casts, and evaluations, and treatments, she was still on crutches, and now in significant chronic pain. The diagnosis was CRPS, an inflammatory disorder of the central nervous system wherein high levels of nerve impulses are sent to the affected area.

In therapy it was revealed that an unconscious seed had been planted early in her softball experience, that her efforts kept the family happy, and possibly in "one piece." The few times her games had been cancelled, she had witnessed anger and agitation in her parents' dynamic with each other. As long as she was playing and the family was watching, all was good. She had the ability and the responsibility to keep everyone okay and the family together. To grow and transition to a new phase that might not allow for the family's regular participation, served to taint what should have been an exciting milestone, a welcomed movement forward in her lifecycle progression. Instead, interpreted as possibly destructive to the family, combined with the reality that she may have wanted to be done with softball, it created the fertile ground necessary for what actually happened. She needed to abandon the movement forward in order to keep the family together, and so she did. She wouldn't go, but it wouldn't be a conscious event.

The family is once again dedicated to her support, but now it is in response to her medical need, as they seek the best "team" of doctors to help her find relief from pain and disability.

DEPENDENCY – THE UNCONSCIOUS DEMAND FOR CONNECTION

Freud talks of the experience of oneness in the womb and the harmony of the early mother/infant connection. The ego perceives a perfect unity, everything as part of itself. The theory suggests that the bliss of this early experience informs efforts throughout our lives. This early connection becomes the unconscious model of unity that we seek in our relationship to the world as well as to ourselves. Inevitably there is a split in this perfect coupling. With healthy development in a responsive and nurturing environment, this separation is accommodated in the process of emotional growth. The expectation of a return to this state accompanies us on our journey through life, sometimes directed toward others, or sometimes toward alternatives in activities, possessions, credentials or success. The more we understand of ourselves and of our experience, the better equipped we are to understand the unconscious influence of our earliest experience, whether positive, negative or in between, and to find healthy connection with the world and with ourselves.

However, if the early experience of attachment and nurturance is problematic (or, all too often, traumatic), efforts to reconnect can become equally problematic. The trauma of abandonment leads to the expectation of continued abandonment. The trauma of cold, rejecting, non-responsive or hostile caregivers leads to the expectation of the same from those closest to us as well as from others. The emotional interpretation one is left with is worthlessness. So how does one successfully connect when the expectation is rejection? Complex and often pathological defenses and compensations develop in order to survive.

In my practice, I see many patients that have become disabled to varying degrees, often seemingly well beyond their years; individuals of all ages presenting complex combinations of symptoms, diseases, and diagnoses. Many live a life suffering unrelenting symptoms but have received no clear diagnosis. They live with chronic pain and/or symptoms of organic dysfunction, maladies of the bones, joints, and spine, and cognitive difficulties of many kinds.

When their story is explored, the extent of their deprivation as children becomes clear. I ask them to describe what they remember of their earliest years. Some remember very little, but nonetheless a pattern emerges in what is remembered. The voices I hear present a variation on the same theme.

"They told me I was a mistake. They were cold, rejecting and critical. I never did anything right. I never felt safe. I was adopted and they regretted it, and they refused to tell me about my real mom. They never told me they loved me. I felt ignored. I felt invisible. They always fought when my dad was drinking. I always felt it was my fault."

"But who brought you today"? I might ask them.

"My mom and dad, I've lived with them my whole life. They do everything for me."

Often in middle age and beyond, they live with their 80 year old parents who continue to care for their every need: transport, meals, hygiene, clothing. The symptoms of the trauma of abandonment find expression in dependency, illness and pain.

Initially, the experience creates an infantile helplessness that is absorbed by forgetting, only to return in physical helplessness down the road, often sooner than later. One might define this journey as attaining a kind of perverse success in finally getting the care that had always been lacking.

We see in our children the efforts made to get needs met, to confirm connection. An acquaintance of mine shared a concern he had with a sudden change in his 3-year-old son's behavior. His young son had started daycare 2 days a week, which was his first experience of care outside the home. While he seemed to be enjoying this new experience very much, the parents noticed a gradual increase in his clinginess over the first few months. Then the nighttime crying began. My friend and his wife chose to be less responsive to the crying in hopes it would take care of itself. Unfortunately the crying soon became a nightly occurrence and in time was accompanied by coughing spells that wouldn't quit. With the embrace of the boy by the mother, in response to his accelerating distress, the coughing and crying would miraculously cease and the child would quickly fall asleep.

Often the quality of a parent's responsiveness increases in proportion to the degree of discomfort or sickness the child is expressing. Humans learn quickly what it might require to receive love and care. And if the effort fails, the result is inevitably disorder on the inside. If this failure is repeated often enough, it will lead to some greater disorder on the outside.

CONCLUSION
Opening to Cure

All pain has an emotional component. Depending upon whether we consciously respond to unavoidable life circumstances in an accepting or rejecting manner will have an impact on our experience. The greater the experience of trauma accompanying pain, the greater the intolerance of that pain. Sudden injury, loss or disease without any anticipation can create intolerable pain. The circumstance and interpretation of pain impacts the experience of the pain. For example, if a soldier in Afghanistan gets shot on a mission but immediately sees it as the means to go home and be with his wife and daughter, the pain may be more tolerable. If once he gets home, and reunited with his family, he finds a job and as a result feels self-respect, the less likely the injury will become a source of chronic pain. On the other hand, if a mother struggling to support a family running a small business is injured or diagnosed with disease and sees as it as the end of her ability to function, the physical pain is more likely to be expressing emotional pain as well and lead to intolerable or chronic pain.

I have worked with thousands of individuals suffering with chronic pain that appears to be out of proportion to the assumed source or that has no clearly defined physical cause. Treatment in the form of pills, shots, and surgery may have been provided but the pain continues. Unconscious interpretations of experience suggesting one is unsafe, not good enough, alone or at fault will create or exacerbate pain.

Self-blame is often a key variable in preventing us from expressing emotional pain emotionally rather than physically. Events in our lives, our own experience of abuse or trauma for example, are often too unbearable to feel directly when informed by guilt; we somehow interpret that it is our fault, so it gets expressed in physical pain.

Although each person's experience is unique, empathy and understanding will lead to certain assumptions about the human emotional experience overall. However, because we function as individuals, we perceive stimuli and feel the complexity of emotion uniquely. No one experiences the "same" circumstance in the same way. Every event is perceived and interpreted uniquely by each individual. Once you consider the complexity of each individual's experience, you realize that although we are all human, each of us lives in and has experienced a different world. And our unique interpretations of that world are affected by our emotional experience from moment to moment.

Psychosomatic symptoms and illness have been documented and understood for a long time. Nonetheless, as contemporary medicine becomes more and more masterful in its scientific applications, it is just beginning to shift its focus in its search for the key sources of chronic pain to a psychological understanding.

So what do we do? The answer lies in taking the risk of opening up to an understanding of our pain. Allowing ourselves to feel what needs to be felt and finally understand. Once we fully understand and FEEL the reality that it is not our fault after all, we find ourselves on the path to cure and finally gain relief and the freedom we deserve.

I have seen it again and again. When longstanding debilitating chronic pain is cured and the trapped energy that has been manifesting as pain is released, former pain patients discover a new identity. They find new, interesting, and fulfilling ways to use their newfound energy. The ways, of course, vary from person to person. Some spend more time with grandchildren, some volunteer more at church, some start new businesses – I had one patient who became a competitive Masters athlete. The human creature, incredible as it is, even tends to completely forget the pain that darkened so many years, "Oh...yeah, I was in pain all that time. I almost forgot."

Life, as it tends to do, begins anew.

REFERENCES

Adler, R.H., Zlot, S., Hurny, C., & Minder, C. (1989). Engel's 'Psychogenic pain and the pain-prone patient': A retrospective, controlled clinical study. Psychosomatic Medicine, 101, 87-101.

Avila, J., & Murray, M. (2011). Prescription Painkiller Use at Record High for Americans. ABC News, 4/20/11.

Breuer, J. & Freud, S. (1895). Studies in Hysteria.

Chapman, C.R., Tucket, R.P., & Song, C. W. (2008). Pain and stress in a systems perspective: Reciprocal neural, endocrine and immune reactions. The Journal of Pain, 9, 122-145.

Darlington, A.S.E., Verhulst, F.C., De Winter, A.F., ... & Hunfeld, J.M. (2012) The influence of maternal vulnerability and parenting stress on chronic pain in adolescents in a general population sample: The TRAILS study. European Journal of Pain, 16, 150-159.

Edwards, C., Whitfield, K., Sudhakar, S., Pearce, M., Byrd, G., Wood, M., ... Robinson, E. (2006). Parental substance abuse, reports of chronic pain and coping in adults. Journal of the National Medical Association, 98, 420-428

Engel, G.L. (1959). "Psychogenic" pain and the pain-prone patient. The American Journal of Medicine, 26, 899-918.

Erikson, E.H. (1959). Identity and the Life Cycle

Garner, B., Eftekhar, A., & Toumazou, C. (2014). Neural control of immunity. Imperial College London, Centre for Bio-Inspired Technology.

Gatchel, R. J., Peng, Y.B., Peters, M.L., Fuchs, P.N., & Turk, D.C. (2007). The biopsychosocial approach to chronic pain: Scientific advances and future directions. Psychological Bulletin, 133, 581-624.

Johnston-Brooks, C.H., Lewis, M.A., Evans, G. W., & Whalen, C.K., (1998). Chronic stress and illness in children: The role of allostatic load. Psychosomatic Medicine, 60, 597-603.

Leader, D., Corfield, D. (2008). Why People Get Sick

Maes, M., Lin, A., Delmeire, L., ... Bosmans, E. (1999). Elevated serum interleukin-6 (IL-6) and IL-6 receptor concentrations in Posttraumatic Stress Disorder following accidental man-made traumatic events. Biological Psychiatry, 85, 833-839.

McEwen, B.S. (2000). Allostasis and allostatic load: Implications for Neuropsychopharmacology. Neuropsychopharmacology, 22, 108-124.

Michna, E., Ross, E.L., Hynes, W., Nedeljkovic, S.S., ... Jamison, R. N. (2004). Predicting aberrant drug behavior in patients treated for chronic pain: Importance of abuse history. Journal of Pain and Symptom Management, 28:3, 250-258

Qiuping, G., Dillon, C., Burt, V.L., (2010). Prescription Drug Use Continues to Increase: U.S. Prescription Drug Data for 2007- 08, CDC NCHS Data Brief, 42

Rapid MRI vs. radiographs for patients with low back pain: a randomized controlled trial. Journal of the American Medical Association, (2003) 289(21): 2810

Sivik, T.M. (1991). Personality traits in patients with acute low-back pain: A comparison with chronic low-back pain patients. Psychotherapy and Psychosomatics, 56, 135-140.

Tietjen, G.E., Brandes, J. L., Peterlin, L., Eloff, A., Dafer, R.M. ... Khuder, S.A. (2009). Childhood maltreatment and migraine (part III). Association with comorbid pain conditions. Headache, 50, 42-51.

The Use of Medicines in the U.S.: Review of 2010, IMS Institute for Healthcare Informatics, April 2011

Wuest, J., Ford-Gilboe, M., Varcoe, C., Lent, B., Wilk, P., & Campbell, J. (2009). Abuse-related injury and symptoms of post-traumatic stress disorder as mechanisms of chronic pain in survivors of intimate partner violence. Pain Medicine, 10, 739.

ACKNOWLEDGMENTS

Many people helped in the creation of this book. I would like to thank my loving wife Angelina, and my children Eitan, Ariel, Nicole and Luke. Thanks to my parents Burt and Barbara Halpern for their lifelong love and support. I am extremely grateful to the physicians who have supported me from the beginning, Dr. Edward Washabaugh III, Dr. John Chatas, Dr. Louis Bojrab, Dr. Jason Brodkey, Dr. Herbert Malinoff, Dr. Mark Weiner, Dr. Dan Berland, and Dr. Thomas Giancarlo. I would like to thank the professors, philosophy teachers and spiritual teachers who formed the foundation of my feelings and perceptions. Thanks to my fellow colleagues with whom I work, including David Gill for his valuable insights, and of course, to my office staff without whom nothing gets accomplished.

.

ABOUT THE AUTHORS

Ross Halpern, PhD is a clinical psychologist who began working with chronic pain patients in 1991, and has performed over 30,000 psychological evaluations.

The author established and maintains a leading psychology clinic in Michigan dedicated to the psychological treatment of chronic pain patients. Dr. Halpern was at the forefront among peers in his early identification and assessment of the opioid epidemic in the mid 1990s, a time when raising this alarm was controversial and seen as a threat to the status quo. Currently he finds himself and his fellow professionals in a medical environment where chronic pain has overtaken heart disease and cancer as the number one medical problem in this country.

The author is considered a leader in the treatment of chronic pain and opioid addiction and regularly advises groups of physicians and insurers on the subject. He regularly works with over one hundred physicians who themselves provide treatment and support to patients with chronic pain.

David Gill is a psychotherapist who has worked with chronic pain patients for the past 12 years. His psychodynamic approach to understanding emotional trauma and its expression in the body provides patients with clarity and relief.